THE LEGACY OF
EMPIRE

THE LEGACY OF EMPIRE

ECONOMIC DECLINE AND CLASS POLARIZATION IN THE UNITED STATES

Berch Berberoglu

New York
Westport, Connecticut
London

Library of Congress Cataloging-in-Publication Data

Berberoglu, Berch.
　　The legacy of empire : economic decline and class polarization in
the United States / Berch Berberoglu.
　　　　p.　cm.
　　Includes bibliographical references and index.
　　ISBN 0-275-93792-5 (alk. paper)
　　　　1. United States—Economic conditions—1981- 2. United States—
Social conditions—1980- 3. Social classes—United States.
4. Working class—United States—Economic conditions. 5. Income
distribution—United States. I. Title.
　　HC106.8.B464　1992
　　330.973′092—dc20　　　91-28778

British Library Cataloguing in Publication Data is available.

Library of Congress Catalog Card Number: 91-28778
ISBN: 0-275-93792-5

First published in 1992

Praeger Publishers, One Madison Avenue, New York, NY　10010
An imprint of Greenwood Publishing Group, Inc.

Printed in the United States of America

The paper used in this book complies with the
Permanent Paper Standard issued by the National
Information Standards Organization (Z39.48–1984).

10 9 8 7 6 5 4 3 2 1

Contents

Tables and Figures

TABLES

FIGURES

Preface

Never before in the recent history of the United States has the future of the U.S. economy been at center stage of debate and discussion as it is today. The internationalization of U.S. capital, which has been taking place ever since the end of the Second World War, has immensely accelerated during the past two decades, and as a result the U.S. domestic economy has begun a process of decline and decay that is now irreversible.

Functioning within the framework of a world economy dominated by U.S. transnationals, the U.S. economy has become a mere appendage of the world production process. Transnational capital, operating according to the logic of the world economy and in the interests of U.S. monopoly capital, is no longer restricted to conducting business within its own original territorial boundaries. Hence it is in this contradictory sense that the dialectics of the internationalization of transnational monopoly capital is leading to the accumulation of great wealth by the U.S. monopolies operating on a world scale, while effecting a decline and decay in the United States itself, bringing about a relative and, in the long run, absolute drop in the standard of living of the vast majority of the American people. Such decline, which has been in effect since the early 1970s, is now threatening to become a permanent feature of life in the United States and thus has immense political implications.

As the great social and political developments of the next decade will, of necessity, be the outcome of the unfolding economic scene in the

United States and the rest of the world, an analysis of the recent transformation of U.S. and world capitalism, within the context of the unfolding accumulation of capital on a world scale, is imperative. It is the urgent need for such an analysis and to draw its necessary political conclusions that in great part has prompted me to undertake this study. I hope that the information and analysis provided in these pages will help illuminate the dynamics of the recent situation in the United States and guide us to understand the developments of the coming period as we rapidly approach the final years of the twentieth century.

A project of this nature involves many years of research and reflection, including the input of countless people and events during its development. My interest in the study of the U.S. economy, state, and society goes back to the mid-1970s, when my analysis of the world economy, imperialism, and the Third World coincided with the U.S. economic crisis of 1974–1975 and my participation in a series of seminars on this crisis at the University of Oregon, as well as at the annual meetings of sociologists and political economists during the latter half of the 1970s and throughout the 1980s.

I would like to thank Larry Reynolds for providing me the theoretical foundations of social analysis that I have come to adopt since the early 1970s, James Petras and Blain Stevenson for helping me place such analysis in an international, global context, and Albert Szymanski for providing the class content of social relations and political struggles. Collectively, they have provided the intellectual (theoretical and methodological) raw materials of my analysis over the years and have led me on the path of discovery of the processes of social, political, and economic developments now underway on a world scale.

As the economic roots of these developments at home and abroad have become all too clear, I have taken upon myself the task of untangling the complex web of social relations that are at base the manifestations of relations of production, distribution, and exchange (i.e., social-economic relations) that ultimately generate, condition, and reinforce or, alternatively, transform the social and political fabric of society. However, given that history is made by human beings, who collectively have the power and/or the determination to greatly affect its course and ultimately preside over it as the agency of social change, it is crucial to understand the dialectical relationship between the social-economic base and the political superstructure in the analysis of the economy, polity, and society. Thus it is possible to study the actions of a given state at the level of politics, and not as a mere reflection of the economy and the class structure in society, despite the fact that political action, as a rule, emerges and develops out of social and economic forces that have developed and matured in society.

Discussion and debate over these theoretical and philosophical questions may seem academic and unrelated to the study of the U.S. and world political economy, but they very much influence, if not determine, one's method and approach to the problem and, consequently, one's analysis and conclusions. In this context, I would like to thank David L. Harvey for his input and discussion on these important issues over the years, as well as Karl Kreplin, Lyle Warner, and Mike Reed, who as friends and colleagues have provided ideas and analyses on issues and events discussed in this book.

I would also like to thank Fikret Ceyhun, David Dickens, Walda Katz-Fishman, Cyrus Bina, Sohrab Behdad, Marty Hart-Landsberg, and Jerry Lembcke for their role in discussions and analysis of the U.S. and world political economy over the past decade.

My thanks also go to Anne Kiefer, my editor at Praeger, for her encouragement and interest in the project and for making the publication of this book possible.

Finally, I would like to thank Denise Schaar for typing many of the tables contained in this book; Tom Snow and Tim MacIntosh for collecting some of the data; as well as the government publications librarians of the University of Nevada, Reno, for their help in locating data.

My wife, Suzan, and my sons, Stephen and Michael, have, as always, provided me much needed encouragement and support to follow through and complete this project; for this and for their unrelinquished love I am eternally grateful to them all.

Introduction

For nearly two decades now the United States has no longer been the foremost world economic, political, and military power that it once was, when it maintained a dominant position on the world scene in the period following the Second World War. As the competition for world supremacy has been unfolding in full speed during the past few decades, new centers of world power have emerged, posing a challenge to U.S. global domination.

Japan, Germany, and other Western European states, on the one hand, and the Soviet Union and China, on the other, have emerged as serious rivals in the economic, diplomatic, and military fields, where the United States is no longer the sole arbiter of global conflicts and crises, as was the case in the 1950s and 1960s. Moreover, in the wake of postwar revolutionary developments in the Third World, the United States, despite its recent massive deployment of military force in the Middle East, is no longer in a position to control events around the world and is relegated to a reactive posture in the face of an irreversible worldwide struggle against imperialism and neocolonialism throughout the Third World.

In Asia, Africa, Latin America, and the Middle East, regions that the United States alone controlled until recently, the U.S. imperial state is more and more forced to seek international diplomatic, military, and financial backing to be able to effectively intervene and affect the course of development in its favor.

The U.S. invasions of Grenada in 1983, of Panama in 1989, and of Iraq in 1991 are an indication of the weakness, not strength, of the U.S. imperial state, which has selected easy targets to flex its muscle with the massive use of military force involving tens of thousands of soldiers (e.g., over 15,000 in the invasion of Grenada, more than 24,000 in the invasion of Panama, and 549,000 in the invasion of Iraq). Such military misadventures, however, are the signs of a superpower in decline—one that is desperate in conveying an image of global strength that is no longer real. It is for this reason that the broad masses of the people in the Third World are more and more rallying behind progressive and revolutionary forces to wage wars of liberation that would finally free them from the stranglehold of imperialism and set the stage for the construction of a new and just society.

In the advanced capitalist world, a "second Marshall Plan" for Europe is now being initiated by the Europeans themselves, as the continent looks beyond 1992 and unfolds its plans for the 1990s and the period beyond the year 2000. Dramatic changes are also taking place in Eastern Europe to complement the rapprochement between the Soviet Union and the European Economic Community (EEC), setting the stage for unity among more and more states on the continent, leading to the formation of a stronger continental alliance that would tip the balance in favor of Europe, thus shifting away from the total reliance on the United States that had been the case throughout the postwar period.

A sense of struggle against economic, political, and military dependence on the United States is being formed in the psyches of the people at all levels of European society, where while the local propertied classes wage economic war against their U.S. counterparts, the middle strata and the working classes are interested in the prospects for change of a national and continental character that would allow for independent social action, while a variety of groups concerned with military, environmental, and cultural issues are taking part in actions that weaken U.S. control and influence in Europe and, conversely, strengthen the foundations of an independent Europe that may yet become a serious contender for world capitalist power, replacing the United States as the leading force in the world political economy. The changes now taking place in Eastern Europe may reinforce this process of seeking independence from the United States, as the combined strength of a new Europe allied with the Soviet Union and Japan may further isolate the influence of the United States in the world economy, hence in the world political situation as well.

As Europe develops into a global superpower during the 1990s and the relative decline of U.S. power around the world continues, the rivalry that is sure to mature between these long-time NATO allies would result in serious consequences for the U.S. economy, polity, and strategic balance that has been the driving force of U.S. postwar dominance of the world political economy over the past several decades.

On the opposite side of the globe, Japan, too, has been waging a full-scale economic offensive, not only carving out a greater and greater share of the world market, but also making inroads into the U.S. economy and financial empire itself. Thus, whereas in the mid-1970s the United States accounted for 6 of the 25 largest commercial banking companies in the world and occupied the top 3 positions, by the late 1980s Japan came to account for 17 of the top 25 banks and occupied the first 9 of the top 10 positions, while there remained only 1 U.S. bank in the top 25 list (*Fortune*, July and August 1975; June 5, 1989, p. 364; and July 31, 1989, pp. 320–321). This represents a major shift in financial power in the world economy and explains the massive flow of Japanese capital to Wall Street and the U.S. economy in general.

With the rapid growth of Japanese business over the past two decades, Japan has thus become a serious contender in the world economy, rivaling the economies of Europe and the United States. While its dependence on oil (supplied largely by U.S. companies) and military control by the U.S. prevents it from becoming an independent military superpower in the foreseeable future, Japan's economic strength and its bilateral and multilateral relations with China, the Soviet Union, and the countries of Western Europe place it in a powerful position where the balance of forces may change in a totally different direction in the 1990s.

Finally, the massive expansion of U.S. transnational capital throughout the world during the past two decades, effecting the transfer of manufacturing production to the Third World, has brought a shift in the U.S. economy from manufacturing to services, thus bringing about a decline in employment, wages, purchasing power, and standard of living of workers in the United States. This has further contributed to the decline of the U.S. economy and ushered in a period of economic crisis that is becoming more and more permanent. While this assessment goes against popular conceptions of a "prosperous" U.S. economy, a careful analysis of developments during the past two decades, particularly during the 1980s, shows that beyond the facade of a "vibrant" U.S. economy there is the reality of continued decline and decay.

While stock market speculation, hostile takeovers, leveraged buyouts, and mergers and acquisitions may soar profits and expand the wealth and fortunes of the few powerful capitalists and their associates, they contribute little or nothing of any concrete value to the bulk of the laboring population and adversely affect the future prospects of the domestic economy. In fact, more and more people are finding out that the gap between rich and poor is growing precisely during an allegedly recovering economy based on short-term superprofits made possible by debt financing. Thus, while the activities of few insiders in this financial chess game yield billions in transferred wealth, which enter the GNP and give us a false sense of recovery, the underlying structure of the national economy is in rapid decline, as the United States loses its industrial base that once provided relatively high-paying jobs—jobs that were the basis of an expanding mass market. With the loss of such jobs, due to plant closings and moving of U.S. corporations into overseas territories or switching to finance, real estate, or services at home, there has been a shift in employment from the manufacturing to the service sector—resulting in a net decline of real wages by a large factor. Such decline in wages of the middle layers of the working class has effectively reduced the mass market and plunged the domestic economy into a permanent crisis. As a result, the United States is now threatened with being reduced to a second-rate economic power whose aggregate wealth and position in the world economy may soon give way to the wealth and power of other, more vibrant capitalist rivals, as the rising GNP of a united Europe, as well as Japan, surpasses that of the United States during the 1990s.

Given the above bleak picture of the U.S. role and position in the world economy and its domestic ramifications, it is not surprising to find many analysts from across the political spectrum, except the most reactionary among them, who proclaim "the end of the American century."

What are the domestic consequences of these world-historical developments that will directly affect millions of working people in the United States? What will the response of capital be to the deteriorating U.S. economic situation? What role will the state play in the unfolding increasingly complex and contradictory process confronting the U.S. economy and society? And what will be the response of organized labor and the working class in general to the growing polarization and class conflict that such a situation is sure to cultivate? It is in an attempt to provide some answers to these and other related questions that we have undertaken the analysis presented in the following pages.

To place our discussion in the proper historical context, we begin our study by examining a number of theories of the rise and fall of global empires in general, and of the United States in particular, which provide some answers to questions concerning the legacy of the U.S. empire and its implications for us today.

Chapter 1

Theories of the World Economy and World Empire

Various attempts have been made to explain the rise and demise of the major world powers from earlier times to the present, and many competing explanations have been provided to account for the success and failure of states that have risen to world prominence and established global empires over long historical periods. The Spanish, the Dutch, the French, the British, and more recently the United States and other global and regional powers since the sixteenth century are cited as dominant world economic, political, and military empires that established themselves as the preeminent centers of the global power structure, with enormous impact on both their rivals and the world at large, as well as their internal economic, political, military, and, ultimately, societal structure. What has been less than satisfactory, however, is the limited answers provided by various theories on the nature and causes of the rise and fall of empires in the world-historical context.

In this opening chapter, we examine a number of different approaches to an explanation of the origins, nature, development, and contradictions of global empires in an effort to delineate the various positions on this question and thus guide us in our attempt to explain the legacy of the U.S. empire in the present global political-economic context.

In broad outlines, we can distinguish three major approaches in studies of the world economy and world empires that attempt to explain the expansion and contraction of the great imperial powers in recent history: (1) the liberal approach; (2) the world system approach; and (3) the class analysis approach. We take up each of these approaches and briefly examine their theoretical positions and methods of analysis within the context of global power relations.

THE LIBERAL APPROACH

The liberal approach to the study of the world political economy is best exemplified by the analysis provided in Paul Kennedy's recent book *The Rise and Fall of the Great Powers*. In it Kennedy makes a compelling argument in favor of a political-military theory of empire within the context of an analysis of global power relations affected by economic changes and their impact on an empire's relative position in the world order.

Referring to the history of the Western powers since the sixteenth century, Kennedy argues that "there is a very clear connection *in the long run* between an individual Great Power's economic rise and fall and its growth and decline as an important military power (or world empire)" (1987, xii, emphasis in the original). For Kennedy, the critical factor determining "the rise and fall of the Great Powers" is that the dominant world powers/empires "steadily overextend themselves in the course of repeated conflicts and become militarily top-heavy for their weakening economic base":

> In these more troubled circumstances, the Great Power is likely to find itself spending much *more* on defense than it did two generations earlier, and yet still discover that the world is a less secure environment—simply because other Powers have grown faster, and are becoming stronger. . . . Great Powers in relative decline instinctively respond by spending more on "security," and thereby divert potential resources from "investment" and compound their long-term dilemma (1987, xxiii).

As a result of such military overextension, which drains productive resources of a nation and brings about an economic decline, a Great Power increasingly runs the risk of being replaced by rival states that do not have such a military burden and are thus in a better economic position to overtake and surpass a declining empire. In fact, it is precisely in this way, according to Kennedy, that shifts in global power centers occur and transformations in the world political economy take place:

> An economically expanding Power—Britain in the 1860s, the United States in the 1890s, Japan today—may well prefer to become rich rather than to spend heavily on armaments. A half-century later, priorities may well have

altered. The earlier economic expansion has brought with it overseas obligations (dependence upon foreign markets and raw materials, military alliances, perhaps bases and colonies). Other, rival Powers are now economically expanding at a faster rate, and wish in their turn to extend their influence abroad (1987, xiii).

Finally, the burden of military spending to maintain a global empire becomes more serious, and the decline and fall of a state from empire status that much more likely, if the state in question is also experiencing a relative economic decline:

If a state overextends itself strategically—by, say, . . . the waging of costly wars—it runs the risk that the potential benefits from external expansion may be outweighed by the great expense of it all—a dilemma which becomes acute if the nation concerned has entered a period of relative economic decline. (1987, xvi)

While without a sufficiently large economic base an empire cannot for long be able to sustain political-military power and remain a dominant force on the world scene, it is ultimately the overextended projection of strategic military force, with all the economic costs it entails and a corresponding decline in the economy itself, that finally brings about the decline and fall of a world empire, according to Kennedy. Thus "a top-heavy military establishment may slow down the rate of economic growth and lead to a decline in the nation's share of world manufacturing output, and therefore wealth, and therefore *power*" (1987, 445)—"a dilemma," Kennedy reminds us, "which becomes *acute* if the nation concerned has entered *a period of relative economic decline*" (1987, xvi, emphases added).

This simple, yet provocative, explanation of the world-historical process confronting the major world powers today—such as the United States, with its large-scale military intervention in the Middle East, precisely at a time when the U.S. economy had entered a deep recession—is both instructive and timely. It also provides a framework for analysis of the U.S. economy and polity and the role of military spending vis-à-vis the structural problems of the U.S. economy and the state in this period of decline and decay.[1]

However, as in other liberal political accounts of the global political economy, Kennedy's approach, focusing as it does on the nation-state as the main unit of analysis, seriously limits our understanding of the nature and causes of global conflicts, rivalry, and shifts in power that can otherwise be more clearly delienated by an analysis of classes and class conflicts lodged in particular nation-states. Restricted to an empirical-descriptive diplomatic history of the world political situation shaped by the general concepts of nations and empires, defined in geographic, political-military terms—albeit affected by economic changes, but divorced from an understanding of the logic of a historically specific dominant mode of production as ultimately determining the nature, scope, and extent of an empire's political-military superstructure and its global dynamics—Kennedy's liberal-institutional approach fails to provide an analysis of the real forces behind the surface manifestations of political behavior of states/empires at the global level.

In the absence of the application of a theory of economic systems to define states in accordance with their social-economic base in production, or, for that matter, any other definition, Kennedy's universalist treatment of states/empires divorced from historical time and space leads him to lump Ming China, Tokugawa Japan, Ottoman Turkey, France, Britain, Germany, the United States, the USSR, and present-day Japan and China, as well as all other major political-military powers, past and present, into the same category, with some—the most powerful and prominent—given Great Power status, without regard to their social-economic systems or relations of production or the class nature of the state.

Kennedy's central argument, revolving around the military element explaining the rise and fall of empires, thus forces him to look at these states in the same way, hoping to find a uniformity of causation in factors contributing to their decline and fall and in the process failing to explain the systemic reasons for each case that is socially and historically specific. By failing to see that global military expansion of the Western powers as a manifestation of economic expansion by the capitalist class internationally and that the internationalization of capital leads to the establishment of global economic domination by the capitalist monopolies, which in turn necessitates the capitalist state to expand its political-military influence and action internationally in order to protect the interests of its capitalist class, thus establishing itself as a global empire, Kennedy characterizes the world order as an "anarchical" one wherein "egoistical" nation-states fight it out in endless wars for world supremacy. Thus, given their common logic—the struggle for power—what determines the success or failure of these states now turned world empires, according to Kennedy, is the degree to which they can balance their military ambitions with the reality of their available economic resources. A disparity between the two, resulting in military overexpansion, is a formula for failure—one that signals long-term decline and demise. The fact that international economic expansion of a given state (which leads to increased military expenditures to defend its global interests) would, in turn, adversely affect its domestic economy on which it depends for further military spending, precisely at a time when the global expansion and relocation of monopoly capital are reducing the size and strength of the domestic economy—hence its ability to support an overextended military on a world scale—is the *real* reason for decline and fall, is not considered by Kennedy as a plausible explanation of the collapse of empires in recent world history.[2]

Starting his analysis in an inverted order, however, Kennedy fails therefore to tell us why an empire would overextend itself militarily in the first place, and inflict upon itself economic disaster, thus running the risk of being replaced by a global rival. One would like to know: Who are the dominant forces that are pushing for such military expansion, and why? Although it may ruin the economy of an entire nation, who are the ones that might benefit from such military expansion? That the logic of an economic system and the class forces that control it may well be the driving force of such action, and not the "preferences," "priorities," or "wishes" of states, as Kennedy would have it, never occurs to him as the decisive factor explaining, in the end, the rise and fall of the Great Powers in the world today.

THE WORLD SYSTEM APPROACH

In contrast to the liberal tradition in political theory, Immanuel Wallerstein provides an alternative, "world system" approach for an analysis of the international political economy. Explaining his method in selecting the world system as the unit of analysis, rather than the nation or the state, Wallerstein argues that he

> abandoned the idea altogether of taking either the sovereign state or that vaguer concept, the national society, as the unit of analysis. I decided that neither one was a social system and that one could only speak of social change in social systems. The only social system in this scheme was the world system (1974b, 7).

"Once we assume that the unit of analysis is such a world system and not the state or the nation or the people," argues Wallerstein, "then much changes in the outcome of the analysis":

> Most specifically we shift from a concern with the attributive characteristics of states to concern with the relational characteristics of states. We

shift from seeing classes (and status groups) as groups within a state to seeing them as groups within a world-economy (1974b, xi).

Going beyond the liberal political tradition and conceptualizing global power struggles as those in accordance with the requirements of a world system that dominates the global political economy over an entire historical period, the world system approach attempts to provide tools of analysis to examine contemporary global political-military developments in the context of the logic of the capitalist world economy that has come to dominate the structure of economic relations on a world scale since the sixteenth century.

The capitalist world economy, defined in terms of market and exchange relations, which binds states under its yoke across the world, brings capitalist and noncapitalist states alike under its sway and determines the nature and course of these states' development as dictated by the most powerful state in control of the world system in a given historical epoch. But competition and rivalry among the leading states engaged in struggle for domination of the world system leave open the possibility that a dominant state in a given historical epoch will be replaced by another:

> While the advantages of the core-states have not ceased to expand throughout the history of the modern world-system, the ability of a particular state to remain in the core sector is not beyond challenge. The hounds are ever to the hares for the position of top dog. Indeed, it may well be that in this kind of system it is not structurally possible to avoid, over a long period of historical time, a circulation of elites in the sense that the particular country that is dominant at a given time tends to be replaced in this role sooner or later by another country (1974a, 350).

Moving beyond nation-states and formulating the problem in world systemic terms, Wallerstein has thus provided an alternative explanation of the rise and fall of world systems, which take place in much longer historical periods and constitute the very basis of world-historical transformations.

In "The Rise and Future Demise of the World Capitalist System," Wallerstein argues in favor of just such a conceptualization in explaining the origins, development, and future transformation of the capitalist world economy and system (1974a). Likewise, situating the problematic in a broader historical context of systemic transformation, Wallerstein elsewhere, in *The Modern World System*, attempts to explain the transition from feudalism to capitalism in Western Europe and the subsequent rise of the capitalist system in such world systemic terms (1974b).

An essential element in the global analysis of the modern world system is the theory's three-tiered model of "core," "periphery," and "semiperiphery," which divides the world system into three areas or zones that are defined on the basis of a society's level of development and incorporation into the world system. Moreover, the political-economic content of such incorporation determines whether a given social formation is part of the core, the periphery, or the semiperiphery (1974a, 1974b).

The organizing principle of this operation is the categorical differentiation of levels of the world-system: core, semiperiphery, and periphery. These zones, distinguished by their different economic functions within the world-economic division of labor . . . structure the assemblage of productive processes that constitute the capitalist world-economy (Hopkins and Wallerstein 1982, 77).

"On a world-scale," continue Hopkins and Wallerstein, "the processes of the division of labor that define and integrate the world-economy are . . . those which we designate as 'core' and 'periphery' " (1982, 45). Moreover, "although obviously derivative from the core-periphery conception," they add, "there exists a third category, structurally distinct from core and periphery": "Looking at the world-economy as a whole, . . . [there exists] a basically triadic world-scale division of labor among, now, core states, semiperipheral states, and peripheral areas" (1982, 47). Thus:

the world-economy became basically structured as an increasingly interrelated system of strong "core" and weak "peripheral" states, in which inter-state relations . . . are continually shaped and in turn continually shape the deepening and expanding world-scale division and integration of production (1982, 43).

This brings up the question of "the network(s) of governance or rule in the area in question." "In this respect," write Hopkins and Wallerstein, "incorporation entails the expansion of the world-economy's interstate system":

Interstate relations, and the interstate system overall, in part express and in part circumscribe or structure the world-scale accumulation/production process. In short, the relational networks forming the interstate system are integral to, not outside of, the networks constitutive of the social economy defining the scope and reach of the modern world-system. . . .

Insofar as external areas are incorporated, then—and in the singular development of the modern world-system all have been—the transition period framing incorporation encloses definite directions of change in a once external area's arrangements and processes of rule or governance (1981, 245–46).

The main feature of the modern world system is, in essence, the transfer of surplus from the periphery to the core of the system, conceptualized in a manner similar to the Frankian "metropolis-satellite" model of domination and "exploitation." The mechanism whereby this transfer takes place is "unequal exchange"—a mechanism made possible by the domination of peripheral states by those in the core:

Once we get a difference in the strength of the state machineries, we get the operation of "unequal exchange" which is enforced by strong states on weak ones, by core states on peripheral areas. Thus capitalism involves not only appropriation of the surplus value by an owner from a laborer, but an appropriation of surplus of the whole-world-economy by core areas. And this was as true in the stage of agricultural capitalism as it is in the stage of industrial capitalism (Wallerstein 1979, 18–19).

More specifically, Wallerstein argues that without this process of "unequal exchange" the capitalist world economy could not exist:

Such a system [of unequal exchange] is *necessary* for the expansion of a world market if the primary consideration is *profit*. Without *unequal* exchange, it would not be *profitable* to expand the size of the division of labor. And without such expansion, it would not be profitable to maintain a capitalist world-economy, which would then either disintegrate or revert to the form of a redistributive world-empire (1979, 71).

Despite the subordination of peripheral states to those in the core, and the exploitation of the former by the latter through surplus extraction, the modern world system allows, under certain conditions and in the context of certain political-economic processes, the transformation of some peripheral states into semiperipheral ones. However, such transformation (or mobility) of states along the three-tiered continuum takes place within the context and logic of the system as a whole and as a consequence of the dictates of the dominant world system in a given historical period. Thus the various parts of the system that make up its totality always function within the framework of the relationship of the parts to the whole.

Although Wallerstein's world system approach is certainly a major improvement over Kennedy's ahistorical eclecticism, it nevertheless suffers from a number of fundamental flaws that must be pointed out. The first, and central, flaw of this approach is the treatment of the world system in strictly circulationist terms. Capitalism, defined as a system of accumulation for profit through the market, is conceptualized in the context of exchange relations. Thus economic relations take place between states within the context of such market exchange. As a result, the question of the mode of production, and its social component, relations of production, is ignored or eliminated from analysis, such that class relations and class struggles based on relations of production also disappear as irrelevant. We are thus left with the generalized abstract notions of "world system" and "world economy" consisting of the three zones (core, periphery, and semiperiphery) between which all the major global relations and conflicts take place. And since changes in any of these three zones, by themselves, cannot bring changes in the world economy or the system as a whole, the system, in all its totality and static abstraction, becomes an end in itself—in effect, an ideal-typical construct studied for its own sake.[3]

Having criticized the Great Powers approach for its universalism and ahistorical eclecticism with regard to the sources of power and politics in the world political economy, we now find ourselves confronting the equally universalist and ahistorical static abstractions of the world systems approach, which has taken us far along an analysis of the broader systemic logic of the capitalist world economy, but not near enough to its class contradictions and conflicts that would provide us the clues to the underlying dialectical class structure and class logic of the empire and its legacy. For this we must turn to the class analysis approach provided by historical materialism.

THE CLASS ANALYSIS APPROACH

In response to the deficiencies of both the liberal-political and world system approaches we have examined above, there has recently emerged a third, alternative approach in critical theorizing on the nature of the state, empire, and imperialism—that of class analysis.

While there are numerous prominent examples of this approach in contemporary political economy surrounding the debate on imperialism and the state on a world scale during the past two decades, we will focus on the analysis provided by Albert Szymanski in *The Logic of Imperialism* as representative of works written in the alternative, class-analysis tradition.

"The motive force behind capitalist imperialism," writes Szymanski, "is found to be the maximization of profits by the transnational corporations that dominate the foreign relations of the major capitalist states" (1981, 123). "These giant corporations and banks," he adds, "are able to transform their tremendous domestic and international wealth into political power, turning the state into an instrument that guarantees their profits" (1981, 147). Thus the international role of the dominant imperialist states is centered on preserving a general climate favorable to profitable investment and trade and is oriented to advancing the interests of the imperialist system as a whole. Moreover, the "various forms of military intervention used by the imperialist states" must, therefore, be seen as "an attempt to ensure the interests of the transnational corporations" (1981, 177). Thus, "to secure the profits of empire . . . a strong world military presence is required that can suppress or intimidate attempts to arouse socialist or nationalist revolutions" (1981, 517). In this way, the supremacy of the imperialist state and transnational capital can be assured throughout the empire.

The relationship between the owners of the transnationals—the monopoly capitalist class—and the imperialist state and the role and functions of this state, including the use of military force to advance the interests of the monopoly capitalist class, thus reveals the class nature of the imperialist state and the class logic of imperialist expansion on a world scale. But, as Szymanski points out, this logic is more pervasive and is based on the logic of a more fundamental class relation between labor and capital that now operates on an international scale, that is, a relation based on exploitation. Thus, in the epoch of capitalist imperialism, "classes," writes Szymanski, "are a product of the logic of the world capitalist system":

> It is the logic of the relationship between the international capitalist class and the working class . . . that is the primary cause of social structures, political forms, and their transformations.
>
> The logic of classes generally explains the actions of nation-states. . . .
>
> Class logic is, in the last analysis, the fundamental integrating force in any world system. . . . [Thus] classes, not nations, must be considered the most fundamental active units of world systems (1981, 15–16).

This position is echoed by James Petras in *Critical Perspectives on Imperialism and Social Class in the Third World*, where he writes:

> The capitalist world market thus must be demystified from a set of static institutions/factors and described essentially for what it is: a series of class relationships that have their anchorage and instrumentation in the imperialist states. The world market operates through the class-directed institutions that impose the exploitative class relationship throughout the world. The world capitalist system can best be analyzed by examining the hegemonic class relationship and imperialist state and conflicting class relationships that emerge in each formation (1978, 39).

Thus, "it is out of these class relationships and the power of the contending classes," Petras writes elsewhere, "that the integration/disintegration of the imperial system originates" (1981, 8). Hence, "the more centrally the class struggle affects the overall functioning of the imperial system, the more absolute dependence between state and class structure":

> The image of the imperial state standing above the class structure that organizes imperialist wars in fact disguises the greatest concentration of social power into the executive agencies of the imperial state and the subordination of civil society to the organized power of the imperial capitalist class (1981, 10-11).

It is for this reason, Petras stresses, that

> the critical problem for analysis is . . . one of examining the conditions under which the process of capital accumulation takes place and its impact on the class structure. Class relations are viewed as a point of departure within which to locate the problem of capital accumulation and expansion (1981, 37).

Explaining the class logic of global capitalist expansion in the twentieth century, "Imperialism," writes Szymanski, "involves the exploitation of the producer or working classes in the dominated country by economic interests based in the dominating country" (1981, 6). And the mechanism that facilitates this exploitation is foreign investment (in raw materials and, increasingly, in manufacturing), which, by way of cheap labor and raw materials, obtains high rates of profit for the transnational monopolies based in the advanced capitalist countries:

Foreign investment is immensely profitable for the transnational corporations. It is in such profitability that the motive behind imperialism is
found. . . .

The tremendous profits made by the transnational corporations in the
raw materials sector (especially petroleum) . . . come mostly from their
monopoly power in the world market. . . .

The rapidly increasing profits made in the manufacturing sector . . . come from the utilization of extremely cheap labor. . . .

In most less-developed capitalist countries authoritarian regimes outlaw
or greatly inhibit strikes, independent unions, and other forms of working
class resistance. Such regimes thus provide the transnational corporations
with both a cheap and responsive labor force (1981, 133–37).

Thus imperialism has been an enormous source of profits and wealth for
the capitalist class of the advanced capitalist countries, who, through the
mechanisms of the transnational monopolies and the imperial state, have
accumulated great fortunes from the exploitation of labor on a world
scale.

Given the uneven development of capitalism, however, some countries
have grown more rapidly than others, while previously less-developed
countries have emerged as new centers of world capitalism. The rivalry
between the capitalist classes of the old and newly emergent capitalist
states has turned into rivalry among the leading countries within the world
capitalist system. This has led to intense competition and conflict between
the rising capitalist powers and the declining imperial centers on a world
scale, hence leading to shifts in centers of global economic and political
power.

The process of world capitalist expansion discussed above has produced a number of major consequences, which are examined at length
in this book and elsewhere (see Berberoglu 1987; 1990; 1992). These
can be listed briefly as follows:

1. the internationalization of capital and the development of capitalism
    and capitalist relations of production in the less-developed countries
    resulting in the superexploitation of a growing working class;

2. the rise of new capitalist centers on the world scene (e.g., Japan,
    Germany, and the EEC), thus leading to interimperialist rivalry;

3. the necessity to protect and police the empire, hence the procurement
    and maintenance of a large number of military bases around the world,
    frequent military intervention in the Third World, the continuing arms
    race, and, as a result, an enormous increase in military spending;

4. decline of the domestic economy and a reduction in the living standard of U.S. workers, leading to increased class polarization; and

5. the class contradictions of imperialism and capitalist development on a world scale, preparing the material conditions for intensified class struggles that lead to revolutionary social transformations throughout the world, including the empire's home base.

Focusing on the U.S. experience, it is clear that in the post–World War II period the United States emerged as the dominant power in the capitalist world. In subsequent decades, U.S.-controlled transnational production reached a decisive stage, necessitating the restructuring of the international division of labor, as the export of productive capital effected a shift in the nature and location of production—the expansion of manufacturing industry on an unprecedented scale into previously precapitalist, peripheral areas of the world capitalist economy. This marked a turning point in the rise to world prominence of the U.S. economy as the United States established itself as the leading capitalist/imperialist power in the world.

Adopting the class analysis approach outlined above, we turn in the next chapter to a detailed analysis of this initial period of postwar growth and expansion of U.S. capitalism on a world scale.

Chapter 2

The Postwar Rise of the U.S. Economy onto the World Scene

There have been two major turning points in the recent economic history of the United States: one marked the rise to world prominence of the U.S. economy at the conclusion of World War II, when the United States came to lead the world economy in the immediate postwar period; the other signaled the end of "the American century" less than three decades later, when the U.S. economy plunged into an irreversible decline in the early 1970s. Thus the period from 1945 to the 1970s has been characterized as the heyday of America's dominant position in the world economy.

THE RISE OF THE U.S. ECONOMY ONTO THE WORLD SCENE

The origin of U.S. capitalist expansion on a world scale goes back to the turn of the century, when U.S. direct investment abroad amounted to nearly a billion dollars, reaching $1.6 billion by 1908; by 1920, it totaled nearly $4 billion (Lewis 1938, 605–6). The post–World War I prosperity, which ushered in the Roaring Twenties, set U.S. capital on its way to a prominent position within the world economy.

Although the Great Depression of the 1930s did dramatically slow down this expansion and greatly affected the rate of growth of the U.S. economy, both domestically and globally, U.S. entry into World War II and the accompanying wartime contracts provided by the U.S. state to the emerging U.S. transnational monopolies in the early 1940s once again propped up the U.S. economy and turned it into a giant productive machine with extensive operations in distant corners of the world. Thus, by 1950, U.S. foreign direct investment reached $12 billion. With the decline of the British Empire and the weakening of the rival European economies in the aftermath of World War II, the United States clearly emerged as the leading center of the capitalist world and came to establish its dominant position as a global superpower. U.S. domination of the world economy and polity in the postwar period went virtually unchallenged for nearly three decades, as both Europe and Japan, as well as most underdeveloped peripheral regions of the world, came under direct U.S. economic and/or political-military control (Szymanski 1981).

During the period since 1950, U.S. foreign direct investment has increased immensely, climbing from $12 billion in 1950 to $124 billion in 1975 to $327 billion in 1988. Together with all other types of investment, total U.S. private investments abroad surpassed $1 trillion in 1988 (see Table 2.1). However, much of this increase was the result of reinvestment of earnings from previous investments, rather than of new capital flows from the United States into the recipient countries (Fajnzylber 1970, 65). In fact, as Table 2.1 shows, outflow of capital from the United States has been only a small fraction of the increase in total foreign direct investment assets. Capital outflows have ranged from $600 million in 1950 to $6.2 billion in 1975, dropping to $300 million in 1986. In 1988, outflow of equity capital reached its lowest level, with a *negative* flow of $5.5 billion. And while direct investment income of U.S. corporations was twice the value of outflows in the 1950s, by 1988 the gap between inflows and outflows reached such vast proportions that it became clear that direct investment income, now totaling about $50 billion, was generated mainly through the internal processes of capital accumulation by the transnational subsidiaries within the host countries. Moreover, U.S. transnational monopolies through this process established a system of transnational production that no longer required the flow of capital from the parent to the subsidiaries for branch-plant expansion.

U.S. economic expansion abroad during this period was a logical outcome of the process of capitalist development in the United States for nearly a century; it also coincided with changes in the global balance of forces that permitted U.S. capital to enter the world stage (Dowd 1977). Thus, while the decline of British and, more generally, European power at the conclusion of World War II provided new opportunities for U.S. capital in previously colonized peripheral regions of the world, it also

Table 2.1
The Growth of U.S. Private Investment Abroad, 1950–1988 (in billions of dollars)

Year	Value of Assets[a]			Direct Investment Flows[b]		
	Total[c]	Long-Term	Direct	Capital Outflow[d]	Repatriated Profits[e]	Investment Income
1950	19.0	17.5	11.8	0.6	1.5	1.3
1955	29.1	26.8	19.4	0.8	2.1	1.9
1960	49.4	44.4	31.9	1.7	2.9	2.4
1965	81.5	71.4	49.5	3.5	5.2	4.0
1970	116.4	103.6	75.5	4.3	7.9	6.0
1975	237.6	174.5	124.1	6.2	18.4	16.6
1980	513.3	291.6	213.5	1.5	42.5	36.8
1985	818.9	371.1	230.3	-2.2	39.8	33.2
1986	935.3	423.6	259.6	.3	46.8	38.4
1987	1,035.4	485.7	308.8	2.5	61.6	52.3
1988	1,120.4	n.a.	326.9	-5.5	59.5	48.3

Notes: [a]At year end; [b]During year; [c]In addition to direct investments, the total figure represents such items as foreign dollar bonds, foreign corporate stocks, and claims reported by U.S. banks (these are all forms of "portfolio" investments); [d]Equity capital; [e]Includes investment income plus royalties, fees, and charges for other services.

Sources: U.S. Department of Commerce, Survey of Current Business (monthly) annual articles on U.S. foreign investment; U.S. Department of Commerce, Selected Data on U.S. Direct Investment Abroad, 1966-1978; U.S. Bureau of the Census, Statistical Abstract of the United States: 1981, p. 833; 1988, p. 758; 1989, p. 776; U.S. Council of Economic Advisers, Economic Report of the President, 1990, p. 409.

opened up vast areas of economic expansion within Europe itself through the Marshall Plan (the rebuilding of Western Europe through extensive U.S. aid).[4]

The Marshall Plan provided an unprecedented impetus for U.S. corporate expansion in Western Europe. It effectively subsidized and promoted the growth and development of U.S. capital in Europe and set the stage for subsequent capitalist expansion throughout the rest of the world. "Since war-torn Europe and Japan were heavily dependent upon U.S. assistance for reconstruction," writes Michael Tanzer,

> the [U.S.] oil companies and the U.S. government used this opportunity to virtually ram American-controlled oil down the throats of the world to replace coal. Thus, Walter Levy, head of the Marshall Plan's oil division, and previously an economist for Mobil, noted in 1949 that "without ECA (the Marshall Plan) American oil business in Europe would already have been shot to pieces," and commented that "ECA does not believe that Europe should save dollars or even foreign exchange by driving American oil from the European market." Some $2 billion of total Marshall Plan assistance of $13 billion was for oil imports, while the Marshall Plan blocked projects for European crude oil production and helped American oil companies to gain control of Europe's refineries (1974, 17–18).

Similarly, the establishment by U.S. capital of large-scale production, distribution, and communication networks on the continent strengthened the hand of the United States in Western Europe and thereby helped U.S. business to dominate the Western European economies throughout the postwar period. Thus U.S. direct investment in Western Europe increased from a mere $1.7 billion in 1950, to $6.6 billion in 1960, to over $25 billion in 1970, to $96 billion in 1980, and to a record $152 billion in 1988 (see Table 2.2).

This expansion by U.S. capital was accompanied by an infusion of other investments into Canada, Australia, Japan, and the less-developed countries of the Third World, which together with investments in Western Europe totaled $327 billion in 1988. Western Europe accounted for nearly one-half of all U.S. direct investments in the world, indicating its central role in the global operations of the U.S. monopolies, especially in the most recent stage of the latter's postwar expansion throughout the world.

To facilitate its economic objectives in Western Europe, U.S. capital utilized the powers of its state to establish a permanent presence there through a military occupation force bolstered by NATO and other instruments of imperial domination and control.[5] In this way, Europe

Table 2.2
U.S. Direct Investment Abroad, by Area, 1950–1988 (in millions of dollars)

	1950	1960	1970	1980	1988
All Areas	11,788	32,744	75,480	213,468	326,900
Developed	6,083	19,456	51,819	157,084	245,498
Western Europe	1,720	6,645	25,255	95,686	152,232
Canada	3,579	11,198	21,015	44,640	61,244
Australia	201	856	3,148	7,584	13,058
Japan	19	n.a.	1,482	6,274	16,868
South Africa	140	286	778	2,321	1,270
Less-developed	5,705	11,319	19,192	52,684	76,837
Latin America	4,735	8,365	11,103	25,964	34,128
Asia	982	1,152	2,260	8,397	18,860
Middle East	n.a.	1,163	1,545	3,310	5,795
Africa[a]	147	639	2,427	2,701	2,898
International	n.a.	1,418	4,469	3,701	4,565

Notes: n.a. = data not available; [a]Excluding Egypt and the Republic of South Africa.

Sources: U.S. Bureau of the Census, *Statistical Abstract of the United States* (various years); U.S. Department of Commerce, *Survey of Current Business* (various issues); U.S. Department of Commerce, Bureau of Economic Analysis, *Selected Data on U.S. Direct Investments Abroad, 1966-78.*

was effectively turned into a colonial outpost of the rising U.S. imperial state at the service of U.S. capital now operating on a world scale. Thus during the immediate postwar period in the late 1940s and early 1950s the United States rapidly established its dominant position in the world political economy and groomed itself as the leading global superpower exerting control and influence throughout much of the capitalist world.

THE ROLE OF THE U.S. STATE IN PROMOTING THE GROWTH AND EXPANSION OF MONOPOLY CAPITAL

An important aspect of the state's supportive role toward capital in this process of global expansion was the close relationship between capital and the state resulting from the granting to U.S. business of lucrative government contracts for war production during World War II. Thus, by 1944, government purchases of goods and services were seven times greater than they had been in 1939. With the onset of the Cold War after the end of World War II, this relationship continued and grew throughout the postwar period. More specifically, in 1958, military purchases accounted for 93.7 percent of the output of the aircraft industry, 60.7 percent of the ships and boats built, 38.5 percent of transportation equipment production, 38 percent of the output of radio and communications equipment industry, 20.9 percent of electrical machinery, 20.1 percent of instruments, 13.3 percent of primary metals production, and 10.4 percent of petroleum output (Nathanson 1969, 211). Focusing on the industrial-commercial electronics industry, we find that

40 percent of all computers installed up to 1959 were purchased directly by the military or by the weapons industry with government funds. In terms of dollar sales, military purchases were even more significant than the 40 percent figure indicates, since they mainly involved large computers. And in one sense, the entire computer market can be traced to the military, since military requirements financed and directed most of the research and development.

What is true for computers applies equally to other large segments of the industrial-commercial electronics market, such as test and measurement equipment and industrial control instruments. Together with computers, these items make up 65 percent of the industrial market. . . .

Altogether then, indirect and direct military demand may account for close to 70 percent of the total output of the $14-billion-a-year electronics industry. This is just the reverse of the market situation in 1950, when consumer products possessed over 60 percent of the market and military products about 20 percent. Since then consumer sales have increased only about $500 million while military sales have increased more than $7 billion (Nathanson 1969, 210).

Clearly it was through such increases in military purchases that a substantial portion of the postwar U.S. economic growth was sustained. Thus, as Paul A. Baran and Paul M. Sweezy point out, "the difference between the deep stagnation of the 1930s and the relative prosperity of the 1950s is fully accounted for by the vast military outlays of the 50's" as the U.S. state came to play a critical role in the growth and development of capitalism in the United States during this crucial period of the rise to world prominence of U.S. monopoly capital (1966, 176). By the mid-1960s, U.S. big business became thoroughly transformed into what Eisenhower had earlier called "the military-industrial complex": 20–30 percent of the annual sales of major electronics firms like RCA, Magnavox, Philco, Sylvania, Motorola, Westinghouse, and General Electric were in the military-space field; others, like Raytheon, Lear, and General Precision Equipment, were selling over 80 percent of their output to the military (Nathanson 1969, 212). Of the 500 largest industrial corporations in the United States in the mid-1960s,

> *at least* 205 [were] significantly involved in military production, either through their primary industry of production, through diversification into the defense sector, or through military research and development contracts. If we exclude from the top 500 the large number of food, apparel, and tobacco firms, then military production involves about 50 percent of the major firms in the economy (Nathanson 1969, 231).

The 1950s and the 1960s thus became the "golden age" of U.S. capitalism—a period that can be characterized as having been a bonanza for big business. The superprofits obtained from overseas investments, government contracts, and intensified exploitation of wage labor at home and abroad resulted in record profits. Except for several short-term downturns in the business cycle, including four major recessions, this period was generally one of growth and expansion, especially for the largest and most viable U.S. corporations. Taking the performance of the 500 largest industrial corporations as a yardstick for the overall sales and profit structure of U.S. big business during 1954–1980, we find that, both in current and constant dollars, sales and profits showed a steady increase during this period (see Figure 2.1). The growth and expansion of U.S. capital during the 1950s and 1960s strengthened the hand of big

Figure 2.1
Sales and Profits of the 500 Largest Industrial Corporations, 1954–1988
(1954=100)

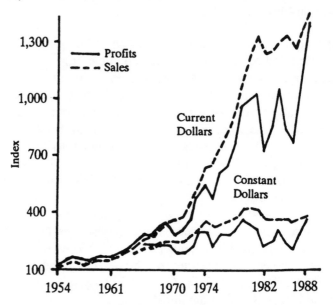

Source: Constructed with data from *Fortune,* April 24, 1989, p. 347.

business and led to the demise of many smaller businesses, thus resulting in the further monopolization of the U.S. economy.

INCREASING MONOPOLY CONTROL IN THE U.S. ECONOMY

The postwar period was a period of accelerated monopolization in the already heavily concentrated and centralized U.S. economy. The process of transnational economic expansion was largely the outcome of the growth and expansion of the giant monopolies in the United States, which, through mergers and acquisitions, came to account for a substantial share of the total assets, sales, and profits during this period (Sherman 1987).

In a report on two decades of economic activity (1954–1974) by the 500 largest industrial corporations in the United States, an analyst for *Fortune* magazine writes: "The conglomerates . . . were rapidly piecing together vast empires of astonishing diversity and, in the process, taking over scores of well-known companies. . . . The merger boom meant, of course, that some companies were scoring tremendous sales gains" (Martin 1975, 239). "Over the course of the two decades," the report continues, "the total annual sales of the 500 leaped from $136.8 billion to $834 billion—an average annual growth rate of 9.5 percent" (1975, 241). It is not surprising, therefore, that the assets of the 500 largest U.S. corporations increased from 55 percent of the U.S. total in 1955, to 75 percent in 1965, to more than 88 percent in 1980; likewise, sales increased from 58 percent of the U.S. total in 1955, to 65 percent in 1970, to 86 percent in 1980; and, finally, profits rose from 45 percent of the U.S. total in 1955, to 54 percent in 1970, to 88 percent in 1980 (see Table 2.3).[6] The latest available data for 1988 give us a further breakdown of this concentration for the top 100, 200, and 500 largest U.S. corporations (see Table 2.4).

In addition to showing continued heavy concentration in sales, assets, and profits for the 500 largest corporations, the data also show that the top 100 corporations accounted for 70 percent of the sales, 74 percent of the assets, and 71 percent of the net profits of the 500 largest corporations, while the top 200 corporations accounted for 85 percent of the sales, 87 percent of the assets, and 85 percent of the net profits of the 500 largest corporations (see Table 2.4). Narrowing the list down to the top 25 industrial corporations and the top 10 financial, banking, insurance, and retailing companies in the United States, we find an even greater level of concentration and centralization of capital at the highest levels of the U.S. corporate structure (see Tables 2.5–2.9).

The 25 largest U.S. industrial corporations accounted for 60 percent of the sales and 68 percent of the assets of the top 100 and 42 percent of the sales and 51 percent of the assets of the top 500 industrial corporations. In banking, the 25 largest U.S. banks accounted for 62 percent of the assets and 59 percent of the deposits of the top 100 banks, while the 10 largest U.S. banks accounted for 40 percent of the assets and 36 percent of the deposits of the top 100 banks. The 10 largest U.S. financial companies accounted for 63 percent of the assets and 58 percent of the revenues of the top 50 financial companies. In insurance, the 10 largest U.S. insurance companies accounted for 61 percent of the assets and 51 percent of the income of the top 50 insurance companies. Finally, in retailing, the 10 largest U.S. retail companies accounted for 56 percent of sales and 61 percent of assets of the 50 largest U.S. retailing companies (see Tables 2.5–2.9).

The process of postwar U.S. monopolization of the economy was not restricted to the industrial, financial, and service sectors alone; agricul-

Table 2.3

Assets, Sales, and Profits of the 500 Largest U.S. Corporations, 1955–1980 (as percent of the U.S. total)

Year	Assets	Sales	Profits
1955	54.6	57.9	44.6
1960	61.0	59.2	43.4
1965	74.9	60.6	40.0
1970	87.8	65.5	53.8
1975	88.1	81.2	56.7
1980	88.6	86.3	88.0

Sources: U.S. Council of Economic Advisers, *Economic Report of the President* (various years); *Fortune* (various issues).

Table 2.4

Sales, Assets, Profits, and Employees of the 100, 200, and 500 Largest U.S. Corporations, by Sales Group Rank, 1988 (in billions of dollars)

Rank by Sales	Sales ($)	Assets ($)	($)^a	Net Profits ($)	($)^a	Employees (Number)
Top 100	1,409.9	1,541.1	(64.3)	81.3	(52.5)	8,333,000
200	1,715.9	1,817.1	(75.8)	97.5	(62.9)	10,635,000
500	2,023.1	2,078.8	(86.7)	115.0	(74.2)	13,144,000

Note: ^{a}Percent of the U.S. total.
Source: U.S. Bureau of the Census, *Statistical Abstract of the United States: 1990*, p. 541.

ture, too, experienced a similar process of consolidation, as fewer and fewer farming units (increasingly formed into giant agricultural conglomerates) came to control a larger and larger acreage, hence a disproportionate share of total assets and cash receipts from farming. In the period 1940–1989 the total farm population decreased from over 30 million in 1940 to less than 5 million in 1989 and the number of farms

Table 2.5
The 25 Largest Industrial Corporations in the United States, Ranked by Sales, 1988 (in millions of dollars)

			Assets	
Rank	Company	Sales	($)	Rank
1.	General Motors	121,085	164,063	1
2.	Ford Motor	92,446	143,366	2
3.	Exxon	79,557	74,293	4
4.	IBM	59,681	73,037	5
5.	General Electric[a]	49,414	110,865	3
6.	Mobil	48,198	38,820	7
7.	Chrysler	35,473	48,566	6
8.	Texaco	33,544	26,337	14
9.	E. I. Du Pont	32,514	30,719	10
10.	Philip Morris[b]	25,860	36,960	8
11.	Chevron	25,196	33,968	9
12.	Amoco	21,150	29,919	11
13.	Shell Oil[c]	21,070	27,169	12
14.	Occidental Petroleum	19,417	20,747	17
15.	Procter & Gamble[d]	19,336	14,820	24
16.	United Technologies	18,088	12,748	25
17.	Atlantic Richfield	17,626	21,514	16
18.	Eastman Kodak[e]	17,034	22,964	15
19.	Boeing	16,962	12,608	26
20.	RJR Nabisco	16,956	17,751	19
21.	Dow Chemical	16,682	16,239	22
22.	Xerox	16,441	26,441	13
23.	USX	15,792	19,474	18
24.	Tenneco	15,707	17,376	20
25.	McDonnell Douglas	15,072	11,885	30
Total for top 25 industrial corps.		850,301	1,052,649	
Total for top 100		1,409,900	1,541,100	
Total for top 500		2,023,100	2,078,800	
Top 25 as % of top 100		(60.3)	(68.3)	
Top 25 as % of top 500		(42.0)	(50.6)	

Notes: [a]Figures include Roper (1987 rank: 389), acquired April 22, 1988; [b]Figures include Kraft (1987 rank: 31), acquired December 7, 1988; [c]Owned by Royal Dutch Shell Group (1987 International 500 rank: 1); [d]Figures are for fiscal year ended June 30, 1988; [e]Figures include Sterling Drug (1987 rank: 174), acquired February 23, 1988.

Source: Compiled with data from *Fortune*, April 24, 1989, p. 354.

Table 2.6

The 25 Largest Banks in the United States, Ranked by Assets, 1988 (in millions of dollars)

			Deposits	
Rank	Company	Assets	($)	Rank
1.	Citicorp	207,666	124,072	1
2.	Chase Manhattan Corp.	97,455	64,057	3
3.	BankAmerica Corp.	94,647	77,150	2
4.	J. P. Morgan & Company	83,923	42,469	7
5.	Security Pacific Corp.	77,870	47,653	5
6.	Chemical Banking Corp.[a]	67,349	47,966	4
7.	Manufacturers Hanover Corp.	66,710	41,714	8
8.	First Interstate Bancorp	58,194	44,149	6
9.	Bankers Trust New York Corp.	57,942	32,491	11
10.	Bank of New York Co.[b]	47,388	32,706	10
11.	Wells Fargo & Co.	47,388	32,706	9
12.	First Chicago Corp.	44,432	32,018	12
13.	PNC Financial Corp.	40,811	27,453	13
14.	Bank of Boston Corp.	36,061	23,591	16
15.	Bank of New England Corp.	32,200	24,623	14
16.	Mellon Bank Corp.	31,153	21,325	19
17.	Continental Bank Corp.	30,578	16,967	30
18.	NCNB Corp.	29,848	20,670	21
19.	First Fidelity Bancorp.	29,777	21,562	18
20.	Suntrust Banks	29,177	23,945	15
21.	Fleet/Norstar Financial Group	29,052	20,701	20
22.	First Union Corp.	28,978	20,033	23
23.	Shawmut National Corp.	28,414	18,988	26
24.	Marine Midland Banks	25,964	17,341	28
25.	Barnett Banks	25,748	22,482	17
Total for top 25 banks		1,347,954	901,195	
Total for top 100[c]		2,161,205	901,195	
Top 25 as % of top 100		(62.4)	(59.2)	

Notes: [a]Name changed from Chemical New York Corp., April 26, 1988; [b]Figures include Irving Bank Corp. (1987 rank: 25), acquired November 29, 1988; [c]Data available for the top 100 banks only.

Source: Compiled with data from *Fortune*, June 5, 1989, pp. 364-78.

declined from 6.5 million in 1940 to little over 2 million in 1989, while the average size of farms rose from 170 acres in 1940 to 456 acres in 1989 (see Figure 2.2). By the late 1980s, the monopolization of U.S. agriculture was so complete that in 1988 less than 15 percent of all farms held 50 percent of all farm assets and received 77 percent of total cash receipts and 85 percent of total net income in farming, while the lowest 34 percent of farms held 10.7 percent of total farm assets and received a mere 1.1 percent of total cash receipts and -1.4 percent of total net

Table 2.7
The 10 Largest Financial Companies in the United States, Ranked by Assets, 1988 (in millions of dollars)

Rank	Company	Assets	Revenues ($)	Revenues Rank
1.	American Express	142,704	22,934	2
2.	Federal Nat'l Mortgage Ass'n.	112,258	10,635	8
3.	Salomon	85,256	6,146	14
4.	Aetna Life & Casualty	81,415	24,296	1
5.	Merrill Lynch	64,403	10,547	9
6.	Cigna	55,825	17,889	5
7.	Travelers Corp.	53,332	18,986	4
8.	ITT	41,941	19,355	3
9.	Morgan Stanley Group	40,051	4,109	16
10.	American International Group	37,409	13,613	6
	Total for top 10 financial companies	714,594	148,510	
	Total for top 50[a]	1,133,720	258,289	
	Top 10 as % of top 50	(63.0)	(57.5)	

Note: [a]*Data available for the top 50 financial companies only.*
Source: Compiled with data from *Fortune*, June 5, 1989, pp. 364-78.

Table 2.8
The 10 Largest Insurance Companies in the United States, Ranked by Assets, 1988 (in millions of dollars)

Rank	Company	Assets	Premium and Annuity Income ($)	Premium and Annuity Income Rank
1.	Prudential of America	116,197	14,397	2
2.	Metropolitan Life	94,232	15,487	1
3.	Equitable Life Assurance	50,416	4,917	6
4.	Aetna Life	48,885	8,266	3
5.	Teachers Insurance & Annuity	38,631	3,065	12
6.	New York Life	35,154	6,929	4
7.	Connecticut General Life	31,096	2,732	15
8.	Travelers	30,672	4,201	9
9.	John Hancock Mutual Life	28,315	4,866	7
10.	Northwestern Mutual Life	25,349	3,542	10
	Total for top 10 insurance companies	498,947	68,402	
	Total for top 50[a]	815,200	133,097	
	Top 10 as % of top 50	(61.2)	(51.4)	

Note: [a]*Data available for the top 50 insurance companies only.*
Source: Compiled with data from *Fortune*, June 5, 1989, pp. 364-78.

Table 2.9

The 10 Largest Retailing Companies in the United States, Ranked by Sales, 1988 (in millions of dollars)

Rank	Company	Sales	Assets ($)	Assets Rank
1.	Sears Roebuck	50,251	77,952	1
2.	K-Mart	27,301	12,126	3
3.	Wal-Mart Stores	20,649	6,360	9
4.	Kroger	19,053	4,614	13
5.	American Stores[a]	18,478	7,010	7
6.	J. C. Penney	14,833	12,254	2
7.	Safeway Stores	13,612	4,372	14
8.	Dayton Hudson	12,204	6,523	8
9.	May Department Stores	11,921	8,144	5
10.	Great Atlantic & Pacific Tea[b]	9,532	2,243	21
Total for top 10 retailing companies		197,834	141,598	
Total for top 50[c]		355,396	233,299	
Top 10 as % of top 50		(55.7)	(60.7)	

Notes: [a]Figures include Lucky Stores (1987 rank: 15), acquired June 2, 1988; [b]Figures are for fiscal year ended February 29, 1988; [c]Data available for the top 50 retailing companies only.

Source: Compiled with data from *Fortune*, June 5, 1989, pp. 364-78.

income. Moreover, nearly 50 percent of all farms held only 16 percent of total farm assets and received a mere 2.5 percent of the total cash receipts and −0.8 percent of total net income (see Figure 2.3).

Overall, in the period 1954–1988 the 500 largest U.S. corporations performed exceedingly well in scoring large gains in sales and profits. Thus, while the aggregate earnings of these corporations increased from 50 percent of total U.S. after-tax nonfinancial profits in 1954 to 75 percent in 1970 and nearly 90 percent in 1988, this occured despite the fact that total sales, as a percentage of GNP, actually *fell* during the 1980s—from 60 percent of GNP in 1980 to 40 percent in 1988 (see Figure 2.4).

This means that the 500 largest industrial corporations have now reached a stage of monopoly wherein a declining volume of sales, relative to the GNP, is generating an increasing share of profits in the economy—a situation that can only be explained by the logic of monopoly.

Figure 2.2
Changes in Farming, 1940–1989

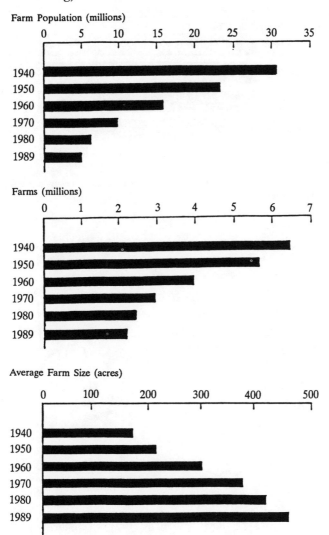

Source: Constructed with data from U.S. Bureau of the Census, *Statistical Abstract of the United States: 1990*, pp. 638-39, and earlier issues.

Figure 2.3
Farms, Farm Income, and Assets, by Value of Sales, 1988

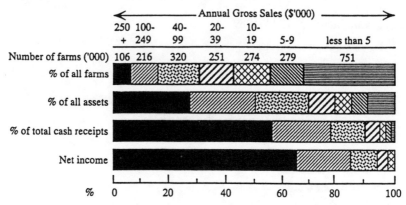

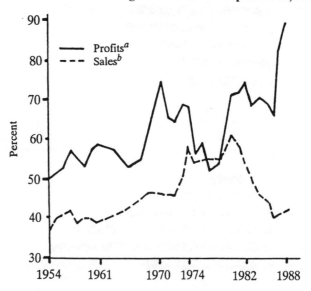

Source: Constructed with data from U.S. Bureau of the Census, *Statistical Abstract of the United States: 1990*, p. 646.

Figure 2.4
Sales and Profits of the 500 Largest Industrial Corporations, 1954–1988

Notes: [a]Profits as percent of after-tax nonfinancial profits; [b]Sales as a percent of GNP.

Source: Constructed with data from *Fortune*, April 24, 1989, p. 347.

NEW CONTRADICTIONS

While the effects of accelerated monopolization in the United States and U.S. transnational expansion abroad began to appear in the U.S. domestic economy as early as the 1970s and became fully visible by the early 1980s, competition from other rival centers of world capitalism began to pose a challenge to U.S. global economic dominance during this period, as a number of rising capitalist states emerged as serious contenders on the world scene. Japan and West Germany, and the EEC as a whole, as well as a number of newly industrializing countries (e.g., South Korea, Taiwan, Hong Kong, and Singapore) began to make headway in production and worldwide trade and together surpassed the traditional U.S. position as the preeminent global economic power in the postwar world economy (Szymanski 1981). Beginning in the opening years of the decade of the 1970s and throughout the subsequent period, U.S. monopoly capital thus began to experience an entirely different process of global economic relations—one that was to set into motion a new set of contradictions which became evident only a decade later.

It is to the analysis of these new contradictions that we turn in the next chapter.

Chapter 3

The Internationalization of U.S. Capital and the Resurgence of Global Rivalry

It is one of the great ironies of our time that imperialism, that is, monopoly capitalism operating on a world scale, would, on the one hand, promote the spread of capitalism throughout the world, while at the same time giving rise to a new set of contradictions at the global and national levels. In this chapter we take up an analysis of the global ramifications of the internationalization of U.S. monopoly capital, while in the next chapter the focus is on the contradictions of this process at the national level.

One major result of the international expansion of U.S. capital during the postwar period, which was intensified and reached unprecedented proportions by the mid-1970s, has been the emergence of new centers of capitalism (Western Europe and Japan) and the resurgence of global, interimperialist rivalry. Such reaction to the postwar domination of the world economy by U.S. monopoly capital has its roots in U.S. entrenchment in the economies of Western Europe and Japan during the past several decades.[7]

THE INTERNATIONALIZATION OF U.S. CAPITAL AND CONTROL OF THE WORLD ECONOMY

U.S. capital, or at least the largest and most aggressive sectors of it, has been operating as part of the world economy ever since the turn of the century. Although still a small power by world standards at that time, the United States entered the world stage long before the disintegration of the British Empire during World War II. Having posed a challenge to Britain's global hegemony and rivaled other European contenders for world power during the years between the world wars, the United States positioned itself to take charge of the capitalist world amidst the ruins and devastation of World War II (Kidron 1970).

Although the large-scale U.S. postwar global expansion ushered in a period of unquestioned U.S. supremacy over the world economy and polity during the 1950s and 1960s, the economic strength of U.S. capital over foreign markets through investment, production, and trade during the 1970s took on a new significance—one resulting from the restructuring of the international division of labor. U.S. transnational capital, in line with its transfer of large segments of the production process to the periphery, poured massive amounts of capital into select areas of the Third World, as well as into its traditional bases of foreign investment—Canada and Western Europe—and became the leading center of world capitalism in a new way, that is, becoming the dominant force in the worldwide production process. Thus not only did overall U.S. direct investment expand immensely during this period, but a shift in the form of investment in favor of manufacturing came to constitute the new basis of changes in the international division of labor (Berberoglu 1987).

As the data in Table 3.1 show, while total U.S. foreign direct investment during 1960–1970 more than doubled, from $32.7 billion in 1960 to $75.5 billion in 1970, it nearly tripled during the 1970s, reaching $213.5 billion in 1980 and $327 billion in 1988. And while petroleum and manufacturing investments accounted for the same proportion of the total, at $11 billion each in 1960, and petroleum investments roughly doubled twice during the following two decades, reaching $19.8 billion in 1970 and $47 billion in 1980, and then $60 billion in 1988, manufacturing investments nearly tripled twice during this same period, reaching $31 billion in 1970 and $89 billion in 1980 and finally reaching $134 billion in 1988 (see Table 3.1).

More significantly, while total aggregate investment dollars in these sectors continued to flow into the developed capitalist countries (primarily Canada and Western Europe), the manufacturing sector of both developed and less-developed countries received a disproportionate share of total investments, far surpassing those in the petroleum industry throughout this period. Thus investments in manufacturing increased from $9.2 billion in 1960, to $25.6 billion in 1970, to $71.4 billion in 1980, to $109 billion in 1988 in the developed capitalist countries and from $1.9 billion in 1960, to $5.5 billion in 1970, to $17.7 billion in

Table 3.1

U.S. Direct Investment Abroad, by Area and Sector, 1950–1988 (in millions of dollars)

Area/Sector	1950	1960	1970	1980	1988
All Countries	11,788	32,744	75,480	213,468	326,900
Mining and Smelting	1,129	3,013	5,405	6,493	n.a.
Petroleum	3,390	10,944	19,754	46,920	59,658
Manufacturing	3,831	11,152	31,049	89,063	133,819
Finance	425	n.a.	7,190	34,405	76,724
Trade	762	2,397	6,201	25,752	34,401
Other	2,251	5,238	5,881	10,835	22,298
Developed Countries	6,083	18,985[a]	51,819	157,084	245,498
Mining and Smelting	411	1,457	3,286	4,487	n.a.
Petroleum	1,251	4,393[b]	11,205	34,173	40,299
Manufacturing	2,984	9,208	25,572	71,399	108,850
Finance	385	n.a.	4,957	20,438	52,577
Trade	472	1,439	4,388	20,548	28,427
Other	580	2,488	2,411	6,039	15,344
Less-developed Countries	5,705	11,319[c]	19,192	52,684	76,837
Mining and Smelting	718	1,556	2,119	2,006	n.a.
Petroleum	2,139	5,326[d]	6,644	10,271	16,007
Manufacturing	847	1,927	5,477	17,664	24,969
Finance	73	n.a.	1,541	13,966	24,146
Trade	325	941	1,318	5,204	5,975
Other	1,603	1,569	2,030	3,573	5,741

Notes: n.a. = data not available; [a]Excluding Japan (data not available); [b]Excluding South Africa and Australia (data not available); [c]Including Japan (data available for Asia as a whole only); [d]Including South Africa (data available for Africa as a whole only).

Sources: U.S. Bureau of the Census, *Statistical Abstract of the United States* (various years); U.S. Department of Commerce, *Survey of Current Business* (various issues); U.S. Department of Commerce, Bureau of Economic Analysis, *Selected Data on U.S. Direct Investments Abroad, 1966-78.*

1980, to $25 billion in 1988 in the less-developed countries (see Table 3.1). Moreover, these investments were concentrated in few key countries within each region: in the developed capitalist world, Canada, Britain, West Germany, and France accounted for the bulk of these investments; and in the less-developed capitalist periphery, Brazil, Mexico, Argentina, Hong Kong, and the Philippines accounted for the bulk of these investments (Berberoglu 1987, 31–40).

These data clearly show a shift in direction from raw materials to manufacturing (and financial) investments throughout the world. As has been the case in the developed capitalist countries for a long time, a number of less-developed countries have reached a stage of economic development where manufacturing investments now represent the single largest category of U.S. foreign direct investment.[8]

In line with this process of expansion in manufacturing investments in Canada, Western Europe, and some regions of the less-developed periphery, U.S. transnational capital has made inroads in acquiring an increasing number of local corporations in these regions in an attempt to reduce or eliminate any resistance to its monopoly of the production, distribution, and accumulation process. Thus we have seen a growing number of U.S. corporate takeovers of prominent European, Japanese, Canadian, Brazilian, and other firms elsewhere in the world during the past two decades in such industries as steel, auto, aerospace, electronics, communications, and banking, to name a few.

With the infusion of large sums of investment into Western Europe beginning in the 1960s, U.S.-based transnationals obtained a dominant position in the European computer and electronics industries by the end of the decade, producing 80 percent of the computers, 95 percent of the integrated circuits, and 50 percent of the semiconductors (Servan-Schreiber 1968, 13–14). Throughout the 1970s the centralization of capital in Western Europe, Canada, and Japan (under U.S. majority ownership and control) intensified, as U.S. firms in other sectors of the economy expanded their operations in a bid to monopolize them as well. Thus by the late 1970s, U.S. foreign direct investment in West Germany reached a predominant position in oil refining (80 percent), glass and cement (54 percent), foods (54 percent), and electrical machinery (51 percent). It also obtained a strong position in iron and metals (50 percent), plastic and rubber (48 percent), pulp, paper, and boards (40 percent), automobiles (37 percent), and chemicals (33 percent), as well as in a number of other sectors, at various rates (Szymanski 1981, 501–2). The United States maintained a prominent position in these investments as the leading country in control of the largest share of the total. As of the late 1970s, among West Germany's 30 largest corporations were nine foreign subsidiaries, of which six (Exxon, General Motors, Ford, IBM, Texaco, and Mobil Oil) were U.S.-owned. Between 1961 and 1978 about 38 percent of all new foreign direct investment in West Germany was from the United States. In Britain, U.S. transnationals obtained an even better position than in West Germany. In 1977 about 110 of Britain's 500 largest nonfinancial corporations were foreign-owned, and two thirds of the total capital invested in Britain by these corporations was controlled by U.S. and Canadian firms.

In Japan, in 1970, of the $7 billion in total foreign assets, the U.S. share was between 60 and 70 percent. U.S. firms accounted for 477 of the 776 foreign companies operating in Japan (Halliday and McCormack 1973, 5). In the early 1970s IBM controlled about 70 percent of Japan's computer market, through a wholly owned subsidiary, the National Cash Register

Company (Japan). In the petroleum industry, foreign capital, predominantly U.S., controlled over half the Japanese market, while the company with the biggest sales of petroleum products in Japan, Nippon Oil Company, was in partnership with the U.S. giant Caltex. By the end of 1971 U.S. capital had control over the supply of 80 percent of Japanese imports of crude oil. And in agriculture, United Fruit Company had moved in late 1971 to raise its holding in the Far East Fruit Company (a joint venture) from 44 percent to 78 percent (Halliday and McCormack 1973, 7). Finally, responding to the expansion of the Japanese car industry into the U.S. market, U.S. car manufacturers, such as General Motors and Chrysler, have moved to buy into the Japanese motor vehicle industry, where General Motors has tied up with Isuzu and Chrysler with Mitsubishi, both capturing over one-third of the stock of these companies, while Ford has captured 25 percent of the stock of Mazda. Thus throughout the 1970s an increasing number of U.S. companies expanded into various branches of Japanese industry (e.g., steel, electronics, high-technology) in an effort to control competitors at the source, while at the same time effecting protectionist measures through high tariffs to seal the U.S. market against the influx of massive imports from rival firms.[9]

In Canada, by the mid-1970s, foreign capital controlled 54 percent of the manufacturing sector, including 69 percent of the electrical products industry, 73 percent of the chemical industry, 92 percent of the petroleum and coal, 67 percent of nonelectrical machinery, and 40 percent of paper and related products. And U.S.-controlled companies accounted for about 75 percent of the total assets of all foreign-controlled corporations (Szymanski 1981, 502).

In Brazil in the late 1970s, foreign firms (mostly U.S.) accounted for the production of 60 percent of heavy machinery, 80 percent of radio and television sets, 90 percent of pharmaceuticals, 95 percent of autos, and 100 percent of tires and rubber products (Berberoglu 1987, 69). The situation is similar in a number of other Third World countries, such as Mexico and Taiwan.[10]

The penetration of U.S. capital into Western Europe, Canada, Japan, and selected Third World countries in the 1970s has resulted in the further centralization of local capital in the hands of U.S. transnationals, effecting greater control over these crucial markets as well as protecting the U.S. market from its competitors, while turning the Western European, Japanese, Canadian, and Third World economies into appendages of a world economy dominated by the U.S. monopolies. In this way, the U.S. transnationals succeeded, by the late 1970s, in dominating the world's production, trade, and financial networks.

Reacting to this situation during the 1980s, Western Europe and Japan have made a comeback to counter the domination of their economies by U.S. capital and thus entered center stage in a new round of global interimperialist rivalry for control of the financial lifeline of the world capitalist economy.

THE RESURGENCE OF GLOBAL RIVALRY IN THE 1980s

The arena of this new rivalry between the major capitalist powers, which began to unfold in full force during the 1980s, extends from Western Europe, to North America, to Japan, to select regions of the Third World, while new areas outside these regions, such as China, Eastern Europe, and the Soviet Union, may become forces that tip the balance in favor of one or another of the capitalist rivals fighting it out on the international scene (see Berberoglu 1992).

The decline of the U.S. economy, beginning in the mid-1970s, coincided with the rise of Europe organized into a viable economic force during this period. The expansion of the EEC via the Common Market on the continent during the 1970s set the stage for the emergence of Western Europe as a serious contender for the leadership of the world capitalist economy. Thus while U.S. capital was in the process of becoming increasingly internationalized and spreading across a vast global territory constituting the new boundaries of a new international division of labor dependent on the U.S. monopolies, Europe focused on its home base in expanding the basis of a giant market of some 400 million relatively well off consumers that would constitute the basis of a mass industrial expansion process that may in the 1990s shift the center of economic power from North America to the European heartland.[11]

A similar development in East Asia and the Pacific Rim brought about the rise to economic prominence of Japan and a number of newly industrializing countries such as South Korea, Taiwan, Hong Kong, and Singapore.

Japan's successful entry into the global economic scene during the past two decades has borne fruit in a big way, as Japanese banks captured, by 1988, a position where 9 of the top 10 banks in the world were Japanese—quite a contrast with the position of Japan in the world economy in the mid-1970s.

In 1974, the 3 largest banks in the world were American (BankAmerica Corporation, Citicorp, and Chase Manhattan) while only 2 of the top 10 banks were Japanese (Dai-Ichi Kangyo, ranked fifth, and Sumitomo, ranked tenth) (see Table 3.2). However, a little over a decade later, in 1988, 9 of the 10 largest banks in the world were Japanese, while only one U.S. bank (Citicorp) remained in the top 25 list. In all, of the 25 largest banks in the world in 1988, 17 were Japanese, 7 were European (4 French, 2 British, and 1 West German), and 1 U.S. (see Table 3.3).

By 1991, all of the top 10 banks in the world were Japanese, while only one U.S. bank remained in the top 25 list. Clearly, by the end of the 1980s and early 1990s Japanese banks came to dominate international finance capital and established themselves as the leading force in the world of finance.

A similar trend in the position of industrial corporations over the past decade and a half has resulted in a decline in number of U.S. corporations and an increase in number of Japanese and European corporations in the

Table 3.2

The 25 Largest Commercial Banking Companies in the World, Ranked by Assets, 1974 (in millions of dollars)

Rank	Company	Country	Assets	Deposits	Rank
1.	BankAmerica Corp.	USA	60,376	50,663	1
2.	Citicorp	USA	57,839	44,742	2
3.	Chase Manhattan	USA	42,532	34,667	3
4.	Banque Nationale de Paris	France	38,418	34,386	4
5.	Dai-Ichi Kangyo Bank	Japan	35,727	23,032	11
6.	Barclays Bank	Britain	33,321	29,249	6
7.	Deutsche Bank	Germany	32,660	30,294	5
8.	National Westminster Bank	Britain	31,884	28,886	7
9.	Credit Lyonnais	France	31,081	28,216	8
10.	Sumitomo Bank	Japan	31,063	20,347	15
11.	Fuji Bank	Japan	30,978	20,169	16
12.	Mitsubishi Bank	Japan	29,337	19,047	19
13.	Bank of Tokyo	Japan	28,960	15,305	24
14.	Sanwa Bank	Japan	28,531	18,063	22
15.	Société Générale	France	28,469	27,203	9
16.	J. P. Morgan & Company	USA	25,963	19,783	17
17.	Dresdner Bank	Germany	25,799	24,036	10
18.	Manufacturers Hanover Trust	USA	25,754	21,513	13
19.	Westdeutsche Landesbank	Germany	23,753	22,364	12
20.	Midland Bank	Britain	23,328	21,198	14
21.	Industrial Bank of Japan	Japan	23,189	18,125	21
22.	Banco de Brazil	Brazil	23,111	18,211	20
23.	Tokai Bank	Japan	22,498	14,272	25
24.	Chemical New York Corp.	USA	22,175	17,814	23
25.	Royal Bank of Canada	Canada	22,009	19,745	18

Source: Compiled with data from *Fortune*, July 1975, p. 116, and August 1975, pp. 164-65.

Table 3.3

The 25 Largest Commercial Banking Companies in the World, Ranked by Assets, 1988 (in millions of dollars)

Rank	Company	Country	Assets	Deposits	Rank
1.	Dai-Ichi Kangyo Bank	Japan	379,323	283,185	1
2.	Sumitomo Bank	Japan	363,233	267,995	2
3.	Fuji Bank	Japan	360,530	258,575	3
4.	Mitsubishi Bank	Japan	348,999	251,147	4
5.	Sanwa Bank	Japan	330,705	246,626	5
6.	Industrial Bank of Japan	Japan	272,918	216,616	6
7.	Norinchukin Bank	Japan	235,944	214,257	7
8.	Tokai Bank	Japan	227,644	172,073	9
9.	Mitsui Bank	Japan	211,359	152,699	15
10.	Credit Agricole	France	210,566	167,104	11
11.	Mitsubishi Trust & Banking	Japan	208,342	178,031	8
12.	Citicorp	USA	207,666	124,072	24
13.	Banque Nationale de Paris	France	196,922	169,887	10
14.	Barclays Bank	Britain	189,251	157,401	13
15.	Bank of Tokyo	Japan	185,429	129,368	22
16.	Long-Term Credit Bank of Japan	Japan	184,753	147,168	19
17.	Sumitomo Trust & Banking	Japan	182,529	162,201	12
18.	Credit Lyonnais	France	178,848	153,745	16
19.	National Westminster Bank	Britain	178,394	153,688	17
20.	Taiyo Kobe Bank	Japan	175,470	131,758	21
21.	Mitsui Trust & Banking	Japan	174,944	151,353	18
22.	Deutsche Bank	Germany	172,143	154,825	14
23.	Yasuda Trust & Banking	Japan	167,848	126,845	23
24.	Société Générale	France	155,457	134,495	20
25.	Daiwa Bank	Japan	150,734	76,790	25

Source: Compiled with data from *Fortune*, July 31, 1989, pp. 320-21.

top 25 list. Thus, while in 1974 15 of the 25 largest industrial corporations in the world were U.S.-based, by 1988 this number was down to 9; conversely, while in 1974 there were only 8 European corporations and only 1 Japanese corporation among the 25 largest industrial corporations in the world, by 1988 these numbers increased to 11 and 4, respectively. Moreover, if we take European and Japanese corporations together as posing a challenge to U.S. dominance of the world economy, we see a complete reversal of the situation in 1988 as compared with 1974. Whereas the share of U.S. corporations in the top 25 list declined from 15 in 1974 to 9 in 1988, the share of European and Japanese corporations increased from 9 in 1974 to 15 in 1988 (see Tables 3.4 and 3.5).

These developments clearly show that a shift in centers of the world economy has taken place during the past two decades—away from the

Table 3.4
The 25 Largest Industrial Corporations in the World, Ranked by Sales,
1974 (in millions of dollars)

Rank	Company	Country	Sales	Assets	Rank
1.	Exxon	USA	42,061	31,332	1
2.	Royal Dutch/Shell Group	Brit./Neth.	33,037	30,194	2
3.	General Motors	USA	31,550	20,468	3
4.	Ford Motor	USA	23,621	14,174	6
5.	Texaco	USA	23,255	17,176	4
6.	Mobil	USA	18,929	14,074	7
7.	British Petroleum	Britain	18,269	15,089	5
8.	Standard Oil of California	USA	17,191	11,640	10
9.	National Iranian Oil	Iran	16,802	6,935	20
10.	Gulf Oil	USA	16,458	12,503	9
11.	Unilever	Britain	13,667	7,116	19
12.	General Electric	USA	13,413	9,369	14
13.	IBM	USA	12,675	14,027	8
14.	ITT	USA	11,154	10,697	12
15.	Chrysler	USA	10,971	6,733	21
16.	Philips' Gloeilampenfabrieken	Neth.	9,422	11,304	11
17.	U.S. Steel	USA	9,186	7,717	18
18.	Standard Oil of Indiana	USA	9,085	8,915	15
19.	Cie Française des Petroles	France	8,909	8,266	16
20.	Nippon Steel	Japan	8,844	9,456	13
21.	August Thyssen-Hutte	Germany	8,664	5,213	25
22.	BASF	Germany	8,497	6,075	23
23.	Hoechst	Germany	7,821	7,795	17
24.	Shell Oil	USA	7,633	6,129	22
25.	Western Electric	USA	7,382	5,240	24

Source: Compiled with data from *Fortune*, May 1975, p. 210, and August 1975, pp. 156, 163.

United States and toward Japan and Western Europe, with Japan controlling the financial lifeline of the global capitalist system and Europe
(especially Germany) and Japan beginning to make inroads into industrial
production.

Finally, in terms of the nature of production, while U.S. and British
corporations engaged in petroleum and motor vehicles production continue to dominate the list, German and Japanese corporations are
concentrated in the production of motor vehicles and high-tech electronics (see Table 3.5).

With the increase in the number of European and Japanese companies
among the top 25, and with production moving in the direction of
advanced electronics, where Japan has clearly achieved an edge over its
U.S. and European competitors, it is not difficult to see that Japanese
financial and industrial capital may well come to dominate the world

Table 3.5

The 25 Largest Industrial Corporations in the World, Ranked by Sales, 1988 (in millions of dollars)

Rank	Company	Country	Sales	Assets	Rank
1.	General Motors	USA	121,085	164,063	1
2.	Ford Motor	USA	92,445	143,366	2
3.	Exxon	USA	79,557	74,293	5
4.	Royal Dutch/Shell Group	Brit./Neth.	78,381	85,681	4
5.	IBM	USA	59,681	73,037	6
6.	Toyota Motor[a]	Japan	50,790	40,818	10
7.	General Electric[b]	USA	49,414	110,865	3
8.	Mobil	USA	48,198	38,820	13
9.	British Petroleum	Britain	46,174	53,030	7
10.	IRI[c]	Italy	45,521	n.a.	-
11.	Daimler-Benz	Germany	41,818	29,282	17
12.	Hitachi[d]	Japan	41,331	49,862	8
13.	Chrysler	USA	35,473	48,567	9
14.	Siemens[e]	Germany	34,129	31,830	15
15.	Fiat	Italy	34,039	40,424	11
16.	Matsushita Electric	Japan	33,922	39,011	12
17.	Volkswagen	Germany	33,696	28,359	18
18.	Texaco	USA	33,544	26,337	19
19.	E. I. Du Pont	USA	32,514	30,719	16
20.	Unilever	Brit./Neth.	30,488	19,893	23
21.	Nissan Motor[d]	Japan	29,097	33,631	14
22.	Philips	Neth.	28,370	25,483	20
23.	Nestle	Switzerland	27,803[f]	22,083	22
24.	Samsung	S. Korea	27,386	22,193	21
25.	Renault[c]	France	27,110	18,185	24

Notes: n.a. = data not available; [a]Figures are for fiscal year ended June 30, 1988; [b]Figures include Roper (1987 rank: 389), acquired April 22, 1988; [c]Government-owned; [d]Figures are for fiscal year ended March 31, 1988; [e]Figures are for fiscal year ended September 30, 1988; [f]Figures include some significant subsidiaries owned 50 percent or less, either fully or on a prorated basis.

Source: Compiled with data from *Fortune*, April 24, 1989, p. 354, and July 31, 1989, p. 291.

economy and establish itself as its center in the decade ahead. This, in conjunction with developments in Western Europe in the early 1990s and the potential economic unity of Eastern and Western Europe during this decade, may bring about a multipolar world economy in which the United States would constitute a junior partner stripped of its postwar dominance, which led our epoch to be characterized as the American century.

The unprecedented economic and political changes unfolding at full speed during the 1980s and early 1990s have ushered in a new international order in which superpower military tensions have given way to global economic competition and rivalry among the leading capitalist economies, which would set the stage for the resurgence of conflicts and struggles between labor and capital on a national and, ultimately, world scale.

To understand the nature and extent of U.S. economic decline in this period of global rivalry—a decline precipitated by postwar U.S. transnational expansion throughout the world—we turn in the next chapter to an analysis of the growing internal contradictions of capitalism in the United States in recent decades.

Chapter 4

Economic Decline and Increasing Class Polarization in the United States

The internationalization of U.S. capital and the restructuring of the international division of labor during the past two decades has plunged the U.S. economy into crisis in a contradictory way: the superprofits obtained from corporate takeovers and acquisitions resulting from the bull market and the mega-mergers of the 1980s have been accompanied by record business bankruptcies, bank failures, the savings and loan crisis, huge trade and budget deficits, declining real wages, and a widening gap between the wealthy and the working class. However, the October 1987 stock market crash, the $500 billion savings and loan disaster in 1989–91, and, more recently, the collapse of the Trump empire have shown the limits of capital accumulation through frenzied speculative financial activity and empire building on the backs of the working people.

As the drive for bigger profits has resulted in large-scale plant closings in the United States and the transfer of the production process to overseas territories, the consequent deindustrialization has led to higher unemployment and underemployment in the United States, pressing down wages to minimum levels (see Harrison and Bluestone, 1988). The contradictions of this process of worldwide expansion and accumulation have brought to the fore new realities of capitalist economics, now characterized by industrial decline and class polarization, accompanied by renewed assault on the living standards of millions of working people in the United States, while a small minority of the corporate rich continues to accumulate great wealth and fortunes from the ever-growing expansion of capitalism on a world scale.

DECLINE OF THE U.S. ECONOMY IN THE 1970s AND 1980s

A number of factors have brought about the decline of the U.S. economy during the past two decades—the ending of the war in Vietnam, the oil crisis, the rise to world prominence of European and Japanese economies (i.e., interimperialist rivalry), the effects of the internationalization of U.S. capital on the U.S. economy, and problems associated with the capitalist business cycle. These, combined with the structural transformation of the U.S. economy in line with its role in the new international division of labor, brought forth in 1974–75 the most severe recession since the 1930s (see Mandel 1980; Sherman 1976). The gravity of the situation in the mid-1970s was such that the post-1975 recovery could not sustain itself for more than a few years, then sank the economy into another recession in 1979–80 and a much deeper one in 1982 (see Devine 1982). While short-term government policies since 1983 have managed to regulate symptoms of the underlying structural defects in the economy and postponed the crisis, the expected big crash in the 1990s may prove to be much worse than any crash previously, for the cumulative impact of the developing capitalist crisis is destined to bring the world economy to a head, especially in its nucleus, the United States.[12]

An examination of the data for the 1970s and 1980s clearly shows the trends, which point to just such an outcome as a likely development in the 1990s. Overproduction of goods resulting in rising inventories, decline in capacity utilization in manufacturing industry, record trade deficits, growing unemployment, decline in real wages and purchasing power, small-business bankruptcies and farm foreclosures, bank failures, a shaky international financial system, record government deficits, and a highly speculative stock market are all grave symptoms of a declining national economy at a time of record corporate profits, mega-mergers, and wholesale acquisitions and takeovers affecting favorably the biggest U.S. corporations (Magdoff and Sweezy 1987).[13]

In examining the data for the past two decades, we see that the continued overproduction of goods in manufacturing and other industries has resulted in ever-larger inventories. Thus, during the period 1970 to 1990, manufacturing inventories nearly quadrupled, rising from $106 billion in 1970, to $311 billion in 1980, to $384 billion in 1990. Similarly, such increases in other sectors of the economy led to a sharp rise in total inventories, from $240 billion in 1970, to $739 billion in 1980, to $1.1 trillion in 1990 (see Table 4.1 and Figure 4.1). This, in turn, has impacted total output, such that cutbacks in production have resulted in a reduction in capacity utilization. Thus, in manufacturing, it fell from 89.5 percent in 1965 to 77 percent in 1971, to 72 percent in 1975, to 70 percent in 1982—during the three consecutive recessions. The decline in durable goods production was even more pronounced, as it fell from 87 percent in 1967, to 73 percent in 1971, to 70 percent in 1975, to 67 percent in 1982 (see Figure 4.2).

Similarly, there was a sharp decline in net private domestic investment during the 1975 and 1982 recessions, falling (in constant 1982 dollars)

Table 4.1
Inventories and Backlogs, 1970–1990 (in billions of dollars)

Year	All Inventories	Nonfarm Inventories		Unfilled Orders
		Manufacturing	Total	
1970	240.3	105.8	209.2	106.2
1971	257.8	107.3	222.4	107.1
1972	285.6	113.6	241.3	121.1
1973	352.6	136.1	287.1	158.9
1974	423.3	177.0	360.9	188.5
1975	428.8	177.8	364.5	172.0
1976	463.3	194.9	403.1	180.6
1977	505.7	210.6	446.4	204.9
1978	588.2	238.4	514.5	262.4
1979	674.8	281.1	594.1	306.5
1980	739.3	310.7	654.8	329.9
1981	789.0	330.2	707.4	327.4
1982	771.5	316.1	692.2	314.3
1983	787.2	315.9	707.8	349.4
1984	858.2	343.4	777.3	372.6
1985	863.5	333.5	792.1	383.2
1986	853.3	321.1	787.0	387.1
1987	920.7	340.8	851.5	421.2
1988	1,004.0	368.6	928.3	468.9
1989	1,055.3	382.7	975.3	504.9
1990	1,062.7	383.7	986.5	515.8

Sources: U.S. Council of Economic Advisers, *Economic Report of the President, 1990*, pp. 314 and 358; U.S. Department of Commerce, *Survey of Current Business*, February 1991, pp. 15 and S-5.

Figure 4.1
Inventories and Backlogs, 1970–1990 (in billions of dollars)

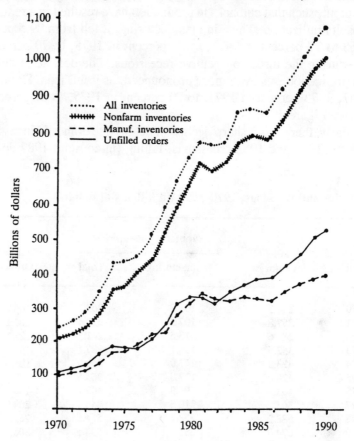

Sources: Constructed with data from U.S. Council of Economic Advisers, *Economic Report of the President, 1990,* pp. 314 and 358; U.S. Department of Commerce, *Survey of Current Business,* February 1991, pp. 15 and S-5.

from $257 billion in 1973 to $96 billion in 1975 and from $253 billion in 1978 to $64 billion in 1982 (see Figure 4.3).

The ups and downs of the business cycle over the past twenty years show that the general trend in business activity is in a downward direction, with each peak lower than the one that preceded it and each trough deeper and worse than what came before. This is also reflected in trends in new housing starts (see Figure 4.4), which further declined as the economy entered another recession in late 1990.

Figure 4.2
Utilization of Manufacturing Capacity, 1965–1990

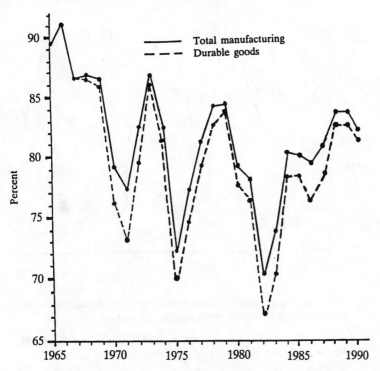

Source: Constructed with data from U.S. Council of Economic Advisers, *Economic Report of the President, 1990*, p. 351; *1991*, p. 343.

While record bankruptcies among small businesses, especially family farms, led to further centralization of the U.S. economy during the recessions of the 1970s and early 1980s (see Meurs 1989, 6–8), the intensified overseas expansion of U.S. transnational monopolies during this period had a serious impact on the U.S. export-import structure as well, resulting in large trade deficits. This came about as a result of a drop in the rate of U.S. exports due to plant closings and a sharp increase in imports from overseas subsidiaries of U.S. transnational monopolies.[14]

As the data in Table 4.2 show, the U.S. trade deficit has greatly increased since the mid-1970s, rising from $9.5 billion in 1976 to $160 billion in 1987. While U.S. transnational expansion abroad continued with exceptional speed during the 1970s, it took on a new significance by the early 1980s, as imports into the United States of manufactured

Figure 4.3
Net Private Domestic Investment,^{a} 1965–1990 (in billions of 1982 dollars)

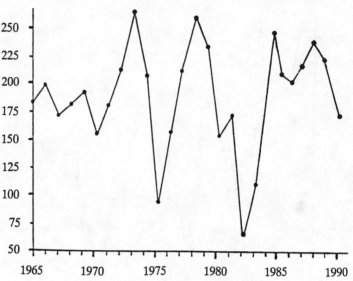

Note: ^{a}Gross private domestic investment less capital consumption allowances with capital consumption adjustment.

Source: Constructed with data from U.S. Council of Economic Advisers, *Economic Report of the President, 1990*, p. 313; *1991*, p. 304.

goods produced by U.S. transnational subsidiaries overseas began to affect the U.S. trade balance in a negative direction beginning in 1982 (see Table 4.2 and Figure 4.5).

Although increased European, Japanese, and other imports are partly responsible for the shift in the balance of U.S. merchandise trade in manufactured goods, the transfer of U.S. productive facilities to cheap labor areas overseas, for the production of goods for sale in the United States, explains in large part the record U.S. trade deficit in recent years (Berberoglu 1987, 47–48).

THE IMPACT OF THE ECONOMIC DECLINE ON THE WORKING CLASS

One consequence of the transfer of the production process to low-wage Third World countries has been a proportionate decline in the U.S. manufacturing work force relative to the total labor force and a commen-

Figure 4.4
New Privately Owned Housing Units Started, 1970–1990 (in millions)

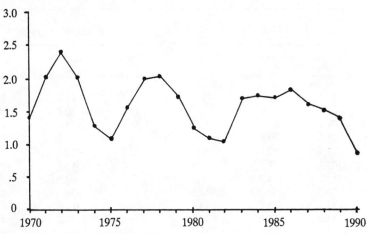

Sources: Constructed with data from U.S. Bureau of the Census, *Statistical Abstract of the United States: 1989*, p. 700; U.S. Council of Economic Advisers, *Economic Report of the President, 1990*, p. 354; U.S. Department of Commerce, *Survey of Current Business*, February 1991, p. C-18.

surate increase in the proportion of low-paid labor in the service sector (see Table 4.3). Thus between 1970 and 1990, the proportion of workers in goods-producing industries declined from 33.3 percent of the labor force in 1970, to 28.4 percent in 1980, to 22.7 percent in 1990; in manufacturing industry, it dropped from 27.3 percent in 1970, to 22.4 percent in 1980, to 17.3 percent in 1990 (see Table 4.4). On the other hand, a segment of the unemployed manufacturing work force that was able to obtain employment in the low-wage service sector accelerated the growth of this sector during the past two decades, such that the proportion of workers in this sector, relative to the total labor force, increased from 66.7 percent in 1970, to 71.6 percent in 1980, to 77.3 percent in 1990 (see Table 4.4).

As the economy has been unable to generate sufficient employment relative to the growth of the labor force in general, there has been a steady increase in the rate of unemployment during this period. And in line with the general trends in the economy over the previous two decades, the unemployment rate has also become a broad indicator of the direction and severity of the economic decline and its impact on the working class in the United States. Thus its rate was 5.8 percent at the height of the 1971 recession, 8.3 percent during the 1975 recession, and 9.5 percent during the 1982 recession; similarly, it was higher at the peak

Table 4.2
U.S. Merchandise Exports and Imports, 1970–1987 (in billions of dollars)

Year	Total			Manufactured Goods		
	Exports	Imports	Balance	Exports	Imports	Balance
1970	42.5	-39.9	2.6	29.3	-25.9	3.4
1971	43.3	-45.6	-2.3	30.4	-30.4	.0
1972	49.4	-55.8	-6.4	33.7	-37.8	-4.1
1973	71.4	-70.5	.9	44.7	-45.0	-1.7
1974	98.3	-103.8	-5.5	63.5	-56.2	7.3
1975	107.1	-98.2	8.9	71.0	-51.1	19.9
1976	114.7	-124.2	-9.5	77.2	-64.8	15.4
1977	120.8	-151.9	-31.1	80.2	-76.6	3.6
1978	142.1	-176.0	-33.9	94.5	-100.3	5.8
1979	184.5	-212.0	-27.5	116.6	-112.2	4.4
1980	224.3	-249.8	-25.5	143.9	-125.1	18.8
1981	237.1	-265.1	-28.0	154.3	-142.5	11.8
1982	211.2	-247.6	-36.4	139.7	-144.0	-4.3
1983	201.8	-268.9	-67.1	132.4	-163.4	-31.0
1984	219.9	-332.4	-112.5	143.1	-221.5	-78.4
1985	215.9	-338.1	-122.2	145.4	-246.8	-101.4
1986	224.0	-368.5	-144.5	148.7	-282.1	-133.4
1987	249.6	-409.9	-160.3	n.a.	n.a.	n.a.

Source: U.S. Council of Economic Advisers, *Economic Report of the President, 1989,*
          p. 426.

of two of the three succeeding recoveries: 4.8 percent in 1973 and 5.8 percent in 1979—dropping to 5.5 percent in 1990, but going up again to 7 percent in early 1991. Black unemployment has followed an identical pattern, but at a much higher level; it increased from 10.4 percent in 1972, to 14.8 percent in 1975, to 19 percent in 1982, at the height of the three succeeding recessions; it was 9.4 percent in 1973 and 12.3 percent in 1979 during two of the three succeeding recoveries—dropping to just over 11 percent in 1990, before going up again to over 12 percent in early 1991 (see Figure 4.6).

Inflation is another factor that impacts negatively the economic position of those dependent on wages and fixed incomes. As U.S. capitalism has developed from its competitive to monopoly stage during the past one hundred years and established itself as the dominant force within the world economy following World War II, inflation has become a permanent feature of the U.S. economy, rising at a steady pace during the past several decades (Sherman 1976). Thus while the peaks in price

Table 4.3
Employment by Industry, 1970–1988 (in thousands)

Industry	1970		1975		1980		1985		1988	
	N	%	N	%	N	%	N	%	N	%
Agriculture	3,463	4.4	3,408	4.0	3,364	3.4	3,179	3.0	3,169	2.8
Mining	516	0.7	752	0.9	979	1.0	939	0.9	753	0.7
Construction	4,818	6.1	5,093	5.9	6,215	6.3	6,987	6.5	7,603	6.6
Manufacturing	20,746	26.4	19,457	22.7	21,942	22.1	20,879	19.5	21,320	18.5
Transportation[a]	5,320	6.8	5,692	6.6	6,525	6.6	7,548	7.0	8,064	7.0
Trade[b]	15,008	19.1	17,713	20.6	20,191	20.3	22,296	20.8	23,663	20.6
Finance[c]	3,945	5.0	4,735	5.5	5,993	6.0	7,005	6.5	7,921	6.9
Services	20,385	25.9	24,174	28.2	28,752	29.0	33,322	31.1	37,043	32.2
Government	4,476	5.7	4,824	5.6	5,342	5.4	4,995	4.7	5,432	4.7
Total[d]	78,678	100.0	85,846	100.0	99,303	100.0	107,150	100.0	114,968	100.0

Notes: [a]Includes communication and other public utilities; [b]Includes wholesale and retail trade; [c]Includes real estate and insurance; [d]The total may not add exactly to 100 percent due to rounding off.

Source: U.S. Bureau of the Census, *Statistical Abstract of the United States: 1989*, p. 391; *1990*, p. 394.

Figure 4.5
Merchandise Exports and Imports, 1975–1987 (in billions of dollars)

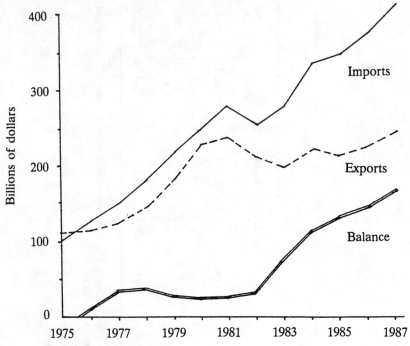

Source: Constructed with data from Table 4.2.

Table 4.4
Workers on Nonagricultural Payrolls, by Industry Group, 1970–1990 (in percentages)

Industry Group	1970	1975	1980	1985	1990
Goods-Producing	33.3	29.4	28.4	25.5	22.7
Manufacturing	27.3	23.8	22.4	19.8	17.3
Service-Producing	66.7	70.6	71.6	74.5	77.3

Source: U.S. Council of Economic Advisers, *Economic Report of the President, 1990*, pp. 342-43; *1991*, pp. 404-5.

rises during the earlier stages of capitalist development in the United States occurred during periods of war—the Civil War, World War I, and World War II (see Figure 4.7)—and were caused mainly by government spending on the military that necessitated the excess printing of money to pay for war-related expenditures, the post-1945 rise in the inflation

Figure 4.6
Unemployment Rate, 1965–1991 (percent of labor force)

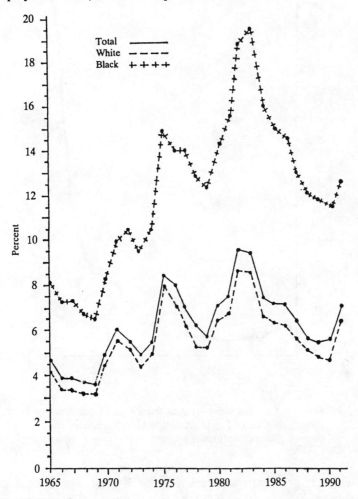

Sources: Constructed with data from U.S. Council of Economic Advisers, *Economic Report of the President, 1990*, p. 339; U.S. Department of Commerce, *Survey of Current Business*, April 1991, p. S-10.

Figure 4.7
Inflation: Consumer Price Index, 1860–1990 (1967 = 100)

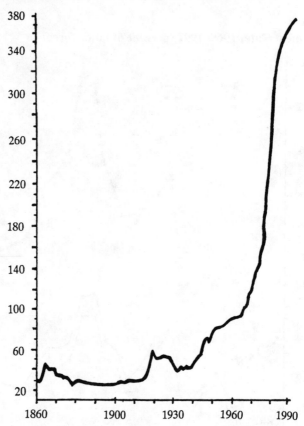

Sources: Constructed with data from U.S. Department of
Labor, Bureau of Labor Statistics; U.S. Bureau of the
Census, *Statistical Abstract of the United States* (various
years).

rate, which in good part was fueled by the Korean War and the war in
Vietnam, was mainly effected by the rise to power of monopoly capital
that could (and did) raise prices at will, without the constraint of
competitive forces in the market—forces that had kept prices in check at
an earlier, premonopoly stage.

With the monopoly structure of the economy in place and in full force,
vertically integrated large corporations, controlling key sectors of the
production, marketing, and distribution network, were able to exert their
power and fix prices at ever-higher levels (Sherman 1976). Thus between

the mid-1960s and late 1980s prices rose by more than 300 percent (see Figure 4.7 and Table 4.5). Most of this increase occurred beginning in the 1970s, when the giant monopolies came to consolidate their position in the economy. During the first half of the 1970s, the rate of inflation averaged 7 percent per year; during the second half of the 1970s, it averaged 9 percent per year, reaching a high of 13.5 percent in 1980 (see Table 4.5).[15]

With increasing unemployment and spiraling inflation during the 1970s and early 1980s, real wages of workers continued to decline, registering

Table 4.5
Inflation and Wages: Consumer Price Index and Average Weekly Earnings of Private Nonagricultural Workers, 1970–1990

| | C.P.I. | | Average Weekly Earnings | | |
| | | | Money Wages | Real Wages | |
Year	(1967=100)	% Increase	Current $	Constant 1977 $	% Change Per Year
1970	116.3	5.9	120	187	-1.3
1971	121.3	4.3	127	191	1.9
1972	125.3	3.3	136	198	4.1
1973	133.1	6.2	145	198	- .0
1974	147.7	11.0	154	190	-4.1
1975	161.2	9.1	164	184	-3.1
1976	170.5	5.8	176	187	1.5
1977	181.5	6.5	189	189	1.2
1978	195.4	7.7	204	189	.2
1979	217.4	11.3	220	183	-3.1
1980	246.8	13.5	235	173	-5.8
1981	272.4	10.4	255	170	-1.5
1982	289.1	6.1	267	168	-1.2
1983	298.4	3.2	280	171	1.9
1984	311.1	4.3	293	173	.9
1985	322.2	3.6	299	170	-1.4
1986	328.4	1.9	305	171	.4
1987	340.4	3.6	312	169	-1.0
1988	354.4	4.1	322	168	- .9
1989	371.4	4.8	335	167	-1.0
1990	391.6	5.4	348	164	-1.6

Sources: U.S. Bureau of the Census, *Statistical Abstract of the United States: 1987*, p. 455; *1988*, p. 385. U.S. Council of Economic Advisers, *Economic Report of the President, 1987*, pp. 293 and 307; *1988*, pp. 299, 313, and 317; *1990*, pp. 344 and 363; *1991*, pp. 336 and 355.

a drop of 7.2 percent during 1974–75 and nearly 12 percent during 1979–1982, covering the last two recessions; during the period 1974–1990 U.S. workers showed a net loss of 18.6 percent in their real income (see Table 4.5).

The sectors of industry most affected by the drop in real wages during this period were retail and wholesale trade, construction, and transportation, while the manufacturing, finance, and service sectors remained stagnant. Overall, average weekly earnings of workers in private industry dropped, in constant 1977 dollars, from $187 in 1970, to $173 in 1980, to $160 in 1990 (see Table 4.6). This is also evident in the drop in real hourly wages since 1978, falling (in 1990 dollars) from a high of $11.40 in 1978 to just over $10.00 in 1990 (see Figure 4.8).

The persistence of income inequality between working men and women during this period made matters worse for women workers, whose income continued to register a big gap in comparison with men's wages, thus perpetuating the added exploitation of women at rates much higher than men. In examining the data on median earnings for 1988 (see Table 4.7), we see that the ratio of women's earnings to men's was .66 for year-round full-time workers and .54 for all workers. The ratio for full-time service workers was .59, for sales workers .57, and for transportation workers .56, while machine operators, assemblers, and inspectors received 62 percent of the wages of male workers in these occupations. The ratios for all workers (including part-time workers) were worse: .57 for machine operators, assemblers, and inspectors, .54

Table 4.6

Average Weekly Earnings of Workers, by Private Industry Group, 1970–1990 (in constant 1977 dollars)

Industry Group	1970	1975	1980	1985	1990
Manufacturing	208	215	212	220	205
Construction	304	300	270	265	243
Transportation[a]	243	262	258	257	234
Wholesale trade	214	206	197	200	191
Retail trade	128	123	108	100	91
Finance[b]	176	167	154	165	166
Services	151	152	140	146	149
Average earnings	187	184	173	170	160

Notes: [a]Includes utilities; [b]Includes insurance and real estate.

Sources: U.S. Bureau of the Census, *Statistical Abstract of the United States: 1990*, p. 407; U.S. Council of Economic Advisers, *Economic Report of the President, 1991*, p. 336; U.S. Department of Commerce, *Survey of Current Business*, April 1991, p. S-12.

Figure 4.8
Real Hourly Wages, 1970–1990 (in 1990 dollars)

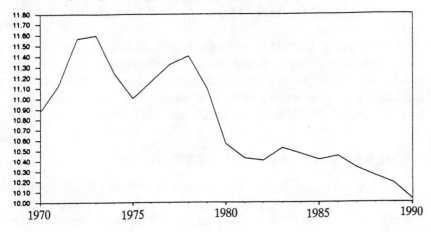

Source: Dollars & Sense, no. 164 (March 1991), p. 23.

Table 4.7
Median Earnings of Workers, by Occupation and Sex, 1988

Occupation	All Workers			Full-time Workers		
	Women	Men	Ratio	Women	Men	Ratio
Service workers	5,181	9,600	(.54)	11,032	18,648	(.59)
Sales workers	6,570	21,795	(.30)	15,474	27,002	(.57)
Machine operators[a]	10,269	18,115	(.57)	13,289	21,382	(.62)
Transport. workers	7,130	19,484	(.37)	13,021	23,453	(.56)
Clerical workers[b]	12,595	18,594	(.68)	16,676	24,399	(.68)
Farm workers	2,439	7,290	(.34)	9,926	14,300	(.69)
TOTAL	11,096	20,612	(.54)	17,606	26,656	(.66)

Notes: [a]Includes assemblers and inspectors; [b]Includes administrative support workers.

Source: U.S. Bureau of the Census, *Statistical Abstract of the United States: 1990,* p. 411.

for service workers, .37 for transportation workers, and .30 for sales workers! (see Table 4.7).

A similar gap in income between white and nonwhite workers became worse by the racist offensive of the 1980s (Melendez 1988, 12–15). While in 1970 black median income was 61 percent of white median income, in the early 1980s it had dropped to 56 percent (Perlo 1988, 98). In 1986, white median family income was more than $29,000, but for blacks it was just over $16,000—that is, 55 percent of white income (Braun 1991, 182).

This enormous race and gender income gap has further contributed to the decline in purchasing power and living standard of U.S. workers during the 1980s: in 1985, the purchasing power of the dollar, as measured by consumer prices in 1967 dollars, declined to its lowest level—31 cents! (U.S. Bureau of the Census 1987, 454).

INCREASING CLASS POLARIZATION

A key factor in the decline in purchasing power and living standard of workers in the United States has been a rise in the rate of surplus value (or exploitation) and a consequent drop in labor's share over the years (Perlo 1988, 35–54). Thus while both production and productivity per labor hour increased continuously during the postwar period, labor's share drastically fell from 40 percent in 1950 to 25 percent in 1984; at the same time, the rate of surplus value in U.S. manufacturing industry doubled from 150 percent in 1950 to 302 percent in 1984 (see Figure 4.9). This, together with favorable government policies toward large corporations (e.g., tax cuts, especially during the past decade), has resulted in record corporate profits. Looking at the past two decades, we find that total net corporate profits more than quadrupled from 1970 to 1988, from $75 billion in 1970, to $200 billion in 1979, to $329 billion in 1988 (see Table 4.8). Likewise, profits of domestic industries increased several-fold during this period, mostly accounted for by nonfinancial industries. Even taking inflation into account—it was quite low in the 1980s—net corporate profits have surged during this period, more than doubling in real terms.[16]

To obtain a more accurate picture of the situation and be able to calculate the rate of surplus value, however, we need to look at gross profits, for net profits hide the amount of total value created by workers that has already been distributed to other segments of the nonlaboring population, such as in the case of corporate executive salaries, federal, state, and local government taxes, and to numerous other industries and commercial enterprises, such as advertising firms. All these deducted business expenses are paid for from the total surplus value created by the workers. Thus, after a detailed analysis of corporate and government data through the mid-1980s, Perlo concluded that both at the aggregate level and at the level of specific corporations "the ratio of gross profits

Figure 4.9
Rate of Surplus Value, U.S. Manufacturing Industry, 1950–1984 (in percent)

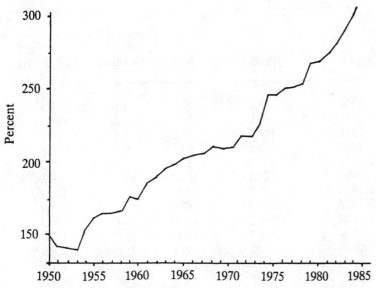

Source: Constructed with data from Victor Perlo, *Super Profits and Crises: Modern U.S. Capitalism* (New York: International Publishers, 1988), Appendix, Table 2A, p. 512.

to net income after taxes was about 5 to 1 or 6 to 1" (1988, 116–17). For example: "The IRS report for all corporations for 1979 shows gross profits (total receipts less cost of sales and other operations) at $1426 billion—almost one and a half *trillion* dollars—compared with net income of $279 billion before taxes and $213 billion after taxes" (1988, 117).[17]

An examination of the extent of concentration and centralization of capital, which reveals the extent of monopolization of the economy and thereby the degree of polarization between social classes, indicates that in 1988 some 334 manufacturing corporations with assets totaling $1.7 trillion and net profits of $112.4 billion accounted for 70 percent of all manufacturing assets and 73 percent of total net profits (see Table 4.9).

While immense wealth has been accumulating in the hands of the wealthy owners of the giant corporations during this period of economic decline and crises, more and more workers have been experiencing a sharp drop in their real wages and standard of living over the past two decades. The resultant growing polarization between labor and capital has thus become crystallized in the distribution of income and wealth in the United States (Braun 1991; Kloby 1991).

Table 4.8

Corporate Profits: Financial and Nonfinancial Industries, 1970–1988 (in billions of current dollars)

Year	Total Corporate Profits[a]	Domestic Industries[b]		
		Total	Financial	Nonfinancial
1970	74.7	62.6	12.2	50.4
1971	87.1	75.1	14.1	61.0
1972	100.7	85.5	15.4	70.2
1973	113.3	92.6	15.8	76.8
1974	101.7	82.4	14.7	67.8
1975	117.6	109.5	11.2	98.3
1976	145.2	139.3	15.9	123.4
1977	174.8	165.5	21.6	143.9
1978	197.2	186.0	29.1	156.8
1979	200.1	180.4	27.8	152.6
1980	177.2	159.6	21.0	138.6
1981	188.0	173.8	16.5	157.3
1982	150.0	131.2	11.8	119.4
1983	213.7	166.6	18.1	148.5
1984	266.9	203.3	13.0	190.3
1985	277.6	193.6	18.4	175.2
1986	284.4	207.2	26.1	181.1
1987	310.4	222.3	30.1	192.1
1988	328.6	238.2	29.8	208.4

Notes: [a]Includes domestic and foreign profits, with inventory valuation and capital consumption adjustments; [b]Includes domestic profits only, with inventory valuation adjustment and without capital consumption adjustment.

Source: U.S. Council of Economic Advisers, *Economic Report of the President, 1989*, pp. 409-10; *1990*, pp. 395-96.

This is evident in data on the distribution of income in the United States over the past two decades. Thus we find that between 1970 and 1987, while the share in total income of the top 5 percent and the highest fifth of families increased, the share of the bottom three-fifths of families decreased (see Table 4.10).

Data on the concentration of wealth in the United States also show the widening gap between the wealthy and the working class in recent decades. Thus, between 1963 and 1983, the richest 10 percent of families have increased their share of total wealth by nearly 7 percent, owning by

Table 4.9
Manufacturing Corporations: Assets and Profits, by Asset Size, 1988 (in millions of dollars)

Asset Size	Number of Corporations	Total Assets		Net Profit	
		$	%	$	%
$1 billion & over	334	1,671,340	(69.7)	112,394	(72.6)
$250 million-$1 billion	550	267,013	(11.1)	14,000	(9.0)
$100-$250 million	729	114,017	(4.8)	5,479	(3.5)
$50-$100 million	783	63,344	(2.6)	3,978	(2.6)
$25-$50 million	494	53,536	(2.2)	3,199	(2.1)
$10-$25 million	972	78,942	(3.3)	4,488	(2.9)
Under $10 million	n.a.	149,750	(6.2)	11,364	(7.3)
All corporations	n.a.	2,397,942	(100.0)	154,902	(100.0)

Source: U.S. Bureau of the Census, *Statistical Abstract of the United States: 1990*, p. 541.

Table 4.10
Distribution of Income in the United States, 1970–1987 (percent of total income received)

Families	1970	1980	1987
Lowest fifth	5.4	5.1	4.6
Second fifth	12.2	11.6	10.8
Third fifth	17.6	17.5	16.9
Fourth fifth	23.8	24.3	24.1
Highest fifth	40.9	41.6	43.7
Top 5 percent	15.6	15.3	16.9

Source: U.S. Bureau of the Census, *Statistical Abstract of the United States: 1981*, p. 438; *1990*, p. 451.

Table 4.11
Distribution of Wealth in the United States, by Ownership of Selected Assets, 1983 (in percent)

Families	Wealth Owned		Real Estate[c]	Corporate Stock	Bonds	Business Assets[d]
	(a)	(b)				
The top .5%	35.1	45.4	35.6	46.5	43.6	58.2
The richest 10%	71.7	83.2	77.8	89.3	90.4	93.6
The remaining 90%	28.2	16.7	22.2	10.7	9.7	6.3

Notes: [a]Distribution of all privately owned wealth, including value of homes owned. The data represent net assets after deduction of debt; [b]The data represent all assets other than homes for personal use, after deduction of debt; [c]Private homes excluded; [d]Includes ownership of interests in unincorporated businesses, farms, and professional practices.

Source: Compiled with data from Joint Economic Committee of the U.S. Congress, *The Concentration of Wealth in the United States*, p. 24, cited in Jerry Kloby, "The Growing Divide: Class Polarization in the 1980s," *Monthly Review* 39, no. 4 (September 1987), pp. 4-6.

1983 nearly 72 percent of all assets, and the top .5 percent of families have increased their share by nearly 10 percent, owning 35 percent of all assets, while the remaining 90 percent of families have experienced a drop in their share of total wealth by nearly 7 percent (Kloby 1987, 7). Moreover, if we exclude from these data homes for personal use, the disparity in wealth becomes even more glaring: in 1983, the richest 10 percent of families owned over 83 percent of all assets and the top .5 percent of families owned nearly half of all assets, while the remaining 90 percent of families owned less than 17 percent of the total. Furthermore, the richest 10 percent of families owned 78 percent of real estate, 89 percent of corporate stock, over 90 percent of bonds, and nearly 94 percent of all business assets. More significantly, the top .5 percent of all families accounted for nearly or over half of all assets, corporate stock, bonds, and business assets (see Table 4.11).

As the process of concentration and centralization of income and wealth moved ahead in full speed during the Reagan years, the continuing class polarization has widened the gap between labor and capital still further and placed the workers into a desperate situation, facing indebtedness, economic uncertainty and fear in securing the basic necessities of life, such as food, housing, and health care, for themselves and for their families.

These and other related concerns documenting the declining living standards of workers in the United States are discussed at length in the next chapter.

Chapter 5

Declining Living Standards of U.S. Workers

We have discussed in the previous chapter the impact of economic decline on the working class with regard to increasing unemployment, declining wages, and the resulting polarization in income and wealth among different segments of the population. In this chapter we examine the overall decline in the living standards of workers in the United States on a number of additional dimensions, including growing indebtedness, the crisis in housing and health care, and increasing impoverishment of the working class. We argue that a general decline in the living standard of the U.S. working class, affecting the material existence of workers on an everyday level, would in turn have a profound negative impact on the structure of the economy itself, thus exacerbating the developing economic crisis.

INCREASING INDEBTEDNESS OF U.S. WORKERS

With the worsening unemployment situation and the declining real wages and benefits of workers in the United States during the past two decades, coupled with price rises—especially affecting food, shelter, and health care—and the consequent decline in real wages, the purchasing power of U.S. workers has dropped considerably during this period of general economic decline (see Chapter 4, Table 4.5). As a result, we have seen during the past two decades a proportionate decline in workers' consumption of basic goods, relative to earlier periods.[18]

To counter their declining real wages and inability to meet their basic needs, many workers have resorted to working overtime or securing a second job, while two-income families in which both husband and wife are forced to work in order to provide for themselves and their children the basic necessities of life, have become more and more the norm. It is not unusual today to find families where not only both spouses work, but children and elderly members of the families as well have taken up paid employment to help pay for their sustenance needs.[19]

An important mechanism of rescuing the economy from the endemic underconsumption crisis, resulting from the declining purchasing power of workers, has been consumer credit. With more and more workers utilizing credit to meet their consumption, shelter, transportation, and other needs, consumer credit has exploded during the past two decades and plunged workers into ever-more indebtedness to the banks and financial institutions, which have in effect enslaved workers in debt bondage. Thus while total consumer credit was $23 billion in 1950 and $60 billion in 1960, in the period between 1970 and 1989 it has increased immensely, from $132 billion in 1970, to $349 billion in 1980, to $729 billion in 1989 (U.S. Council of Economic Advisers 1990, 382). This, together with all other types of credit extended to workers to supplement their income and increase their purchasing power, has led to an enormous rise in household debt as a percentage of after-tax income between 1975 and 1988—from 71 percent in 1975 to 94 percent in 1988 (see Figure 5.1). Thus, by the late 1980s, "the average U.S. household owed nearly the equivalent of its entire annual after-tax income,"[20] while by early 1990

at least 65% of U.S. households are in debt, either with a mortgage or a consumer loan, and 55% have zero or negative net financial worth: they owe more than they own in financial assets. . . .

With living standards thus threatened, low- and middle-income households have become increasingly dependent on credit to continue buying a relatively stable amount of goods and services. In other words, the majority of households have taken on more debt since the early 1970s not so they can spend more, but because they are fighting to avoid consuming less (Pollin 1990, 9–10).

The increasing indebtedness of working-class households has placed them in a position where more and more members of the family must work to pay off debt and prevent foreclosure of their homes or avoid the possibility of personal bankruptcy over unpaid medical bills should a catastrophic illness strike the family:

Figure 5.1
Household Debt as Percentage of After-Tax Income, 1965–1988

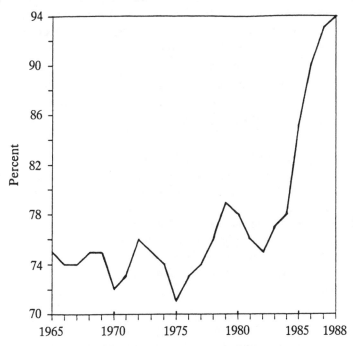

Source: Flow of Funds Accounts of the Federal Reserve
System, cited in *Dollars & Sense*, no. 156 (May 1990), p. 11.

Recent evidence confirms that households are indeed facing growing
repayment difficulties. For example, delinquencies on mortgage loans
have risen throughout the 1970s and 1980s, reaching a new peak of 6.6%
in 1989, from only 2.9% in 1969. Mortgage foreclosures and household
bankruptcy rates have also risen sharply in recent years (Pollin 1990, 10).

Millions of workers who have lost their jobs, or have been unable to
locate one, and could not secure credit to obtain the things they need to
survive have thus been thrown into poverty, some even finding themselves
among the growing number of homeless.[21]

THE CRISIS IN HOUSING

Obtaining adequate housing to shelter one's family has become a
critical concern for millions of workers in the United States in recent

decades. "During the 1950s," writes Robert Parker, "about two-thirds of all U.S. families could have afforded the average new house without spending more than 25 percent of their income," but by the early 1970s this ratio "dropped to one-half and by the early 1980s, fewer than one in ten families could afford the average new dwelling without devoting more than 25 percent of their income on housing" (1991, 173).

Over the past two decades the housing crisis has been manifested in a large number of workers unable to qualify for a home loan or unable to make the down payment necessary to secure a loan.

> In 1975, the average new single-family home cost $44,600. Assuming a standard 8.75 percent loan, a 20 percent down payment, and housing costs at 25 percent of income, a family needed to make a down payment of nearly $9,000 and would have had monthly payments of $280. In contrast, the average price of a new home in 1988 was around $120,000. Assuming a 30 year mortgage and an interest rate of 10 percent, a home purchaser would need an annual household income of about $50,000, and an additional $30,000 on hand to cover the down payment and closing costs (Parker 1991, 173).

One of the main reasons for the inability of workers to obtain adequate housing has been the rising cost of buying and maintaining a house. As a result, the percentage of families able to buy a house has been declining since 1970. Thus while in 1970 the median price of a new single-family house was $23,400, which 46 percent of U.S. families could afford at the time, by 1974 the price had climbed to $35,900, reducing the percentage of families able to afford it down to less than 30 percent, and by 1980 it had jumped to $64,600, with less than 5 percent of families able to afford it! (see Figure 5.2). By 1985 the price of such homes increased to $85,000, and by 1988 it was over $112,000 (see Figure 5.3). According to the National Association of Realtors, the median price of a new home is projected to surpass $125,000 by the early 1990s.[22] It is no wonder that the purchase of a new home has been well beyond the reach of most workers in the United States in recent decades. Especially hard hit are young workers and their families: in the period 1973–1987, the proportion of homes owned by young families headed by those under 25 fell from 23 percent to 16 percent (Curran and Ranzetti 1990). In the past, first-time home buyers have accounted for nearly half of annual housing purchases; in the early 1980s, only about 13 percent of the homes sold were to first-time home buyers (Feagin and Parker 1990, 218).

Figure 5.2
Percentage of U.S. Families Able to Afford Median-priced New Houses,
1970–1980

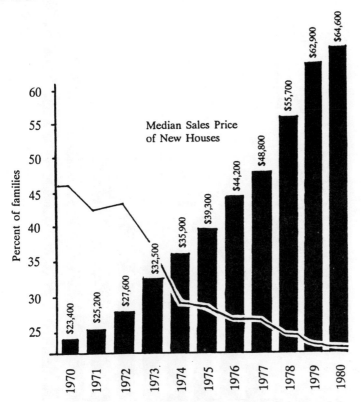

Sources: Constructed with data from U.S. Bureau of the
Census, *Statistical Abstract of the United States: 1990*, p. 716;
U.S. Department of Housing and Urban Development,
Construction Reports.

"Rising home prices and interest rates, along with stagnating income
levels," states another report, "were the consequences of an economy in
the initial stages of crisis."

As inflation picked up steam in the 1970s, mortgage interest rates steadily
followed suit. . . .

Moreover, rising home prices far outpaced income gains. Between 1968
and 1984, median home prices increased 40% faster than the income of
the buyers of those houses. Higher home prices, in turn, required larger
down payments from buyers. Thus in 1968, a 20% down payment on the

Figure 5.3
Median Sales Price of New Houses, 1980–1988 (in thousands of dollars)

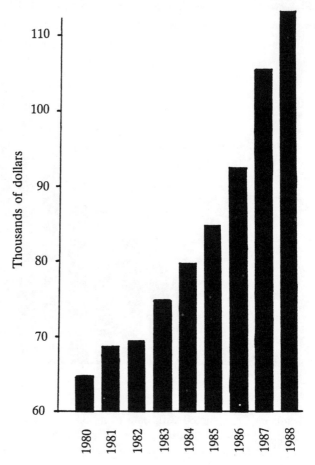

Source: Constructed with data from U.S. Bureau of
the Census, *Statistical Abstract of the United States:*
1990, p. 716.

typical home amounted to 32% of the income of the typical buyer; by
1984, that same 20% down payment ate up 50% of the buyer's income.

The result has been a significant decline in housing affordability and
the homeownership rate, continuing even into the so-called recovery years
of the mid-eighties. Today, fewer households are able to afford the median
priced home, and those that can must spend more of their income to do
so (*Dollars & Sense* 1986, 10).

Earning insufficient wages and unable to afford the monthly mortgage payments or having purchased homes but, due to the loss of a job or other economic difficulties, losing their homes through foreclosure, millions of workers have thus been left out of the housing market, where the struggle to obtain and maintain a shelter for one's family has become more acute in recent decades.[23] In the face of such difficulties, most workers have resorted to renting a house, a mobile home, or an apartment and have found themselves in constant struggle with landlords in trying to pay their monthly rent with an ever-shrinking source of income. "The affordability problem that vexes potential homeowners," Parker points out, "similarly affects renters": comprising over one-third of all households in the United States, renters find themselves in an especially vulnerable position due to the housing squeeze, having no alternative but to devote some one-third to two-thirds of their income to making rent payments (1991, 173). A number of studies have shown "the extra hardship borne by renters, the poor, and minorities . . . [as] nearly 70% of poverty-level renters paid more than half of their income for rent in 1987" (cited in Parker 1991, 174).

Given this situation, low-income, run-down public housing in packed conditions has been the only available source of shelter for many workers in big cities across the country. But even here, as the development and construction of low-income housing is not as profitable as that for high-income groups, there has been a general decline in the availability of such housing while the need for it has increased. As Lynn Shields points out,

Low-rent housing is harder than ever to find and to hang on to. The Reagan years have capped a decade and a half of increasing hardship for low-income renters, decimating the supply of affordable housing. The result is a shelter crisis the likes of which this country hasn't witnessed since the Great Depression (1988, 9).

A closer examination of the deteriorating housing situation during this period reveals:

Between 1974 and 1983, the number of low-rent housing units (those renting for less than $250 per month) dropped by more than one million, while the number of units renting for more than $400 increased by four and one-half million. Meanwhile, demand grew apace; the number of households in need of low-rent housing increased by roughly 3 million (Parker 1991, 173).

The situation deteriorated further throughout the 1980s, and according to Shields, "the worst is yet to come":

> By most projections, the long-term inability of the private sector to meet low-income housing needs, coupled with slashed federal housing programs in the 1980s, portends a future shock in affordable housing. Homelessness in the 1980s could be the calm before the storm (1988, 9).

With growing unemployment and the bleak prospects of finding a good job, a growing number of low-wage, part-time, unskilled young workers and their families are more and more finding themselves in the streets and in shelters for the homeless.

During the decade of the 1980s homelessness has grown immensely. Data published by the Institute for Research on Poverty place the number of homeless in the United States at between 2 and 3 million (1987–88, 20–24). Contrary to the generalized public misconception that the homeless population in the United States is mostly comprised of the mentally ill, Parker tells us that a large segment of the homeless is made up of the working poor: in some cities, he reports,

> more than half of the homeless have jobs. . . . One survey of 12 homeless shelter operators found (without exception) not just more families among the homeless, but more families where a member is working as a maid, a dishwasher, a security guard, or some other job that pays too little to provide shelter (1991, 177).

Clearly one of the major causes of homelessness and its accelerated growth in the 1980s is the declining earning power of workers resulting from changes in the labor force structure (away from manufacturing jobs to minimum-wage service jobs), which is compounded by growing unemployment and underemployment in various sectors of the economy.[24]

The deterioration of health care in the United States is another aspect of this multilayered process of declining living standards of U.S. workers in recent decades.

THE CRISIS IN HEALTH CARE

The biggest problem in obtaining minimum health care by workers in the United States has been the lack of health coverage for workers who have lost their jobs—especially those among the 83 percent of the labor force who do not belong to a union. As more and more large corporations have moved to low-wage Third World countries, such as Mexico, South Korea, and Taiwan, the closing down of plants in the United States has further exacerbated the unemployment situation, thus affecting not only the ability of workers to earn a living, but also the status of their health, as the loss of a job has also meant the loss of all health benefits. This has contributed greatly to the deterioration of the general health of workers in the United States over the past two decades.

Workers who have been able to hold onto their jobs, on the other hand, have not always had access to medical care, as a substantial number of those in the work force have no medical coverage, including millions of part-time workers who are not eligible for employer-provided medical benefits:

> In the late 1980s only about 60 percent of all employers offered group health insurance to their employees. While approximately three-quarters of all Americans are covered by private (nongovernment) health insurance, the number drops to just over half for black Americans and less than one-third for families with low incomes. . . . Today . . . a major operation and a week or two in a hospital can cost many thousands of dollars and wipe out the savings both of poor and of middle-income families, even if they have private health insurance (Feagin and Feagin 1990, 216).

One of the major contributing causes of the rise in medical costs is the sharp increase in hospital costs. According to the Census Bureau, the average daily hospital room charges in the United States have gone up from $83 in 1976, to $127 in 1980, to $262 in 1989; the average cost of hospitalization per day has gone up from $151 in 1975, to $245 in 1980, to $539 in 1987; and the cost of an average hospital stay has risen from $1,164 in 1975, to $1,851 in 1980, to $3,850 in 1987—an increase of 216, 257, and 231 percent respectively in little over a decade (U.S. Bureau of the Census 1981, 111; 1990, 107). In all, total personal health care expenses have increased enormously—from $65 billion in 1970, to $220 billion in 1980, to $443 billion in 1987, a 581 percent increase in just 17 years; of these, the amount paid out-of-pocket by consumers has risen from $43 billion in 1970, to $136 billion in 1980, to $281 billion in 1987—a 553 percent increase over the same 17-year period (U.S. Bureau of the Census 1990, 93).

At a time when the workers' real wages have been falling some 18 percent over the past decade and a half, these huge increases in health care costs have become a serious concern for workers and their families. Alarmed by this situation, "Why has the cost risen so sharply?" asks Alexander Liazos. His answer: "Simply, medical care has become a very profitable big business. Doctors, corporations that make drugs and supplies, hospitals, and nursing homes are all reaping huge profits" (1982, 280). "Large, profit-seeking medical technology corporations," write Joe R. Feagin and Clairece Booher Feagin, "have accelerated the trend toward the bureaucratization and high cost of American medicine":

> High-technology medicine is the result of a long series of important decisions disproportionately made by the officials of large corporations, professional medical societies, and corporate foundations, decisions resulting in an impersonal, highly technological, drug-oriented medicine pervaded by the drive for private profit and private control over the health care system (1990, 244).

High doctors' fees, expensive equipment, supplies, and drugs manufactured by few large corporations, exorbitant hospitalization charges, compounded by unnecessary surgery, tests, and office visits, all of which facilitated by guaranteed insurance and government payments to doctors, hospitals, and other providers, are responsible for the sharp rise in medical costs, hence for the continuing crisis of health care in the United States. The result of this private, profit-centered structure of the U.S. health care system is a situation where profits come first and people and their well-being last—and then, only if they can pay for it!

INCREASING IMPOVERISHMENT OF U.S. WORKERS

Declining real wages, reduced purchasing power, growing indebtedness, inability to afford decent housing and health care, and a general decline in living standards of workers in the United States during the past two decades have led to increasing impoverishment of the working class both in relative and absolute terms. This situation is now threatening the very survival of millions of workers in providing their families adequate food and shelter to sustain life at the subsistence level.[25]

The official poverty level for a family of four in 1983 was $10,178. But more than half of the 8 million new jobs created between 1979 and 1984 paid less than $7,000 a year. This means that more than half of the jobs created during this period "did not cover even the minimum costs of the physical reproduction of workers unless those earning such a low wage had a working spouse" (Gimenez 1987, 23).

An often overlooked factor accounting for the increase in poverty in the United States during the past decade, Jerry Kloby points out, "is the low wages that so many of today's jobs pay":

> In the past few years there has been a dramatic increase in the number of people who work but still fall below the poverty line. The number of persons age 22 to 64 who work but are still poor has increased by more than 60 percent since 1978. Likewise, the number who work full-time year round and are still poor stands at 2 million. That is double what it was in 1978. The number of people who work but are nearly poor is also increasing (1991, 50).

Millions of workers finding themselves at such minimum levels of subsistence have joined the ranks of the impoverished population that has become a permanent fixture of contemporary American society. "Lacking access to the material conditions for their physical and social reproduction on a daily and generational level," writes Martha Gimenez,

> over 32 million members of the working class below the poverty level barely survive under the restrictive conditions imposed by the welfare state. Altogether, 43.4 million people live below 125 percent of the poverty level; this includes 9.4 million families (45.9 percent headed by women) and 15.5 million children under 18 (51.1 percent of which live in families headed by women) (1987, 25).

The situation was worse in the 1980s than it was in the 1970s, such that "the number of poor people went up by one-third between 1978 and 1987, a rate three times the rate of growth for the population" (Braun 1991, 149). Thus while persons below the poverty level numbered about 25 million during the 1970s, this had increased to about 32 million during the 1980s. Of these, nearly 10 million were black and over 22 million were white,[26] while Hispanics, who may be of either race, numbered 5 million (U.S. Bureau of the Census 1990, 458).

Considering the population living below 125 percent of the poverty level, we find that in the 1970s some 35 million people were in this category, while in the 1980s this number climbed to about 44 million. Of these totals, nearly 12 million were black and 32 million were white (U.S. Bureau of the Census 1990, 459).

In proportionate terms, however, only 10 percent of whites were below the poverty level in 1987, while for blacks this rate was 33 percent—more than three times the rate for whites. Likewise, while less than 15 percent of the white population found itself below 125 percent of the poverty level, more than 40 percent of blacks found themselves below this level (U.S. Bureau of the Census 1990, 459).

There has been a very large growth of children living under poverty: "more than one in five children were living under poverty in 1987" (Braun 1991, 151). The rate for black children was 45 percent, and for children living in female-headed households it was 55 percent. In absolute numbers, however, there were nearly twice as many (7.6 million) white children in poverty as there were black (4.3 million) (U.S. Bureau of the Census 1990, 459).

Clearly, a large segment of the working class is seriously affected by poverty, and the effects of racism and sexism have compounded the deteriorating situation of working women and minority workers, who have come to suffer disproportionately from the increasing impoverishment of the working class as a whole.

Chapter 6

The Response of the U.S. State to the Social and Economic Crisis

Historically, the state in capitalist society has played a central role in facilitating the accumulation of capital and its regulation across different industries and sectors of the economy. This was true in the early stages of capitalist development in Europe and the United States in the eighteenth and nineteenth centuries, as it is today, when the state is deeply involved in the domestic and global political economy.

Through what has become known as Keynesian policies, the postdepression, postwar modern U.S. state has expanded its role as an instrument of capital accumulation and as the guardian of the capitalist system in the United States and other allied states around the world.

While the position and role of the U.S. state has become increasingly intertwined with the broader capitalist political economy and the interests of capital in particular, prompting some to identify the system as "state monopoly capitalism" (Perlo 1988), the instrumentality of the state to capital and the capital accumulation process has taken on a new turn, with new and far-reaching consequences for the U.S. economy and society during the past decade.[27]

REAGANOMICS: THE POLITICAL ECONOMY OF DECLINE AND FALL OF EMPIRE

In the early years of the Reagan administration, when the policies of the U.S. state began to unfold into what came to be known as "Reaganomics," Frank Ackerman wrote:

One company after another is enjoying newly won tax breaks, regulatory rollbacks, and employee concessions on wages and work rules. These corporate conquests rest in large part on the actions of the Reagan administration. Ronald Reagan's policies amount to an insistence that the crisis of the U.S. economy can only be solved on terms dictated by big business (1982, 137).

During this period of deregulation and state-sponsored arms buildup,

generals and military contractors rejoiced at the shift of funds from civilian agencies to the Pentagon. Upper-income tax payers enjoyed the particular biases of the Reagan tax cut. Corporate polluters breathed more freely thanks to deregulation (Ackerman 1982, 2).

In short, "Reaganomics" came to be understood as "militarization of society and impoverishment of the working population":

A no-nonsense projection of U.S. power abroad; getting the government out of social services and further into buying high-profit, high-technology hardware; driving down wages, working conditions and taxes; ending "environmental extremism"—all this, the story goes, is supposed to make it attractive for corporations to start investing and growing again (Ackerman 1982, 138).

In fact, just the opposite was the result: investment dropped, the economy began to decline, and the United States plunged in 1982 into the deepest recession since the Great Depression.

While the Great Depression of the 1930s had necessitated active government intervention in the economy and society to help restore minimum living standards, provide public funding to promote economic growth, and pull the country out of a severe economic crisis, the conservative policies of the Reagan administration during the 1980s were claimed to have aimed at achieving the same ends by less government and less interference in the workings of the market. This apparent reversal in long-standing government policy toward the economy in place since the Great Depression, however, turned out to be more of a rhetoric intended to justify huge tax cuts for the rich and a rationalization for cuts in social spending than a real turnaround in state policy with respect to its supportive role toward big business, as we learned from the confessions of the administration's chief spokesman on budgetary policy, David Stockman (see Greider 1981).[28]

The granting of lucrative contracts to defense firms through increased military spending and borrowing of enormous sums from the big banks at high interest rates to pay for the shortfall in revenues, which resulted in big budget deficits throughout this period, are important aspects of the promilitary, big-business-oriented policies of the Reagan administration.

In line with these policies, the United States in the 1980s "established the main components of a war economy in a time of formal peace" (Perlo 1988, 307). With military procurements in the Reagan years reaching the highest point since World War II,

> an important proportion of the major U.S. industrial and financial corporations have had a large profit stake in the inflated and expanding military budget. And added to these prime contractors are literally tens of thousands of subcontractors, many of whom have found that military orders have provided the difference between profitability and bankruptcy. . . .
>
> The top-heavy military budget has been promoted, in the main, by the dominant sections of the capitalist class, which have profited enormously from it, even those with little direct military business. . . .
>
> The militarization of the economy and the foreign policy accompanying it have been major, if not the most important, factors enabling capital to make gains at the expense of labor (Perlo 1988, 315–18).

Thus while increased military spending and the militarization of society have resulted in greater profits for a handful of armaments contractors that are among the largest industrial corporations in the United States,

> the growth of federal government expenditures, the fuel for the remilitarizing of the economy, has continuously outstripped the growth of federal government revenues, drastically reduced by a prorich cut in taxes on individual income and corporate profits. The result has been unprecedented peacetime deficits that have more than doubled the total public debt in less than a decade (Miller 1987, 237).

As a result, during the 1980s "we have lived through the worst economic conditions since the Great Depression":

> a severe contraction followed by a hollow recovery (led by military spending and consumption, not investment), the deindustrialization of our economy and the decline of the international competitiveness of its basic industry, financial exhilaration mixed with financial crises, a widening

gulf between rich and poor, and a dramatic increase in the incidence of poverty (Miller 1987, 237).

Clearly, the policy in place during the Reagan years was one designed to transfer wealth from the working class and the poor to the rich, where the right-wing big-business-controlled state ushered in an era of reaction—ranging from an all-out assault on labor, to reversals in civil rights and the rights of women and other sectors of the population, to an agressive resurgence of global military interventionism.

Far from its detachment from the economy, society, and polity, the state under the Reagan administration was fully involved in all spheres of social life, especially in the economy—on the side of capital, on the side of the rich! The results of this process of "Robin Hood in the reverse" proved to be disastrous for the economy, for the country, and, above all, for the working class and the poor:

> United States policies of the 1980s . . . [have promoted] short-term prof-itability (the production of surplus value) at the expense of the reproduction of the productive capacity of the economy, the reproduction of the conditions of everyday life for the working class, and even the reproduction of the state itself (a fiscal crisis of the state) (Miller 1987, 237).

The U.S. state thus entered a period of unprecedented peacetime budgetary crisis—a crisis that resulted in an extraordinary growth of total national debt and a parallel growth in the amount of the net interest on debt.

THE FISCAL CRISIS OF THE STATE

In the early 1970s, James O'Connor (1973) drew our attention to the state's budgetary crisis and pointed out the political implications of this crisis for labor and society in general. Since then, the fiscal crisis of the state has become much deeper and much more serious on all fronts. As the size of the government has grown and its expenditures increased, in direct proportion to the state's global imperial obligations to transnational capital, so have military spending, state subsidies to business, and other functions to preserve and protect the capitalist system. This, coupled with the supply-side policies followed during the past decade, has resulted in large annual budget deficits and an enormous increase in the total national debt, climbing to $3.2 trillion in 1990 (U.S. Office of Management and Budget [OMB] 1991, Part 2, p. 287).[29]

"In the class analysis of political economy," writes John Miller, "the content of the state budget . . . is a matter of vital importance":

> Every government budget is a "class-budget" and the spending it commissions must be evaluated in light of its effect on the standard of living of the working class and its effect on the profitability of capitalist investment. The content of the state budget has a profound effect on the ability of state intervention to restructure the conditions for profitable investment by the capitalist class and on the impact of state spending on the everyday life of the working class (1987, 239).

Similarly, as the primary sources of the state's revenues are taxes collected from individuals and corporations, "the most crucial question is the class incidence of taxation; who bears the burden of financing the state—capital or labor?" (Miller 1987, 240).

Let us take a closer look at (1) the budget priorities of the state during the 1980s, by way of examining the allocation of funds for various categories of public spending; and (2) the sources of state revenue during this period, to see *who* has been paying *how much* for these expenditures.

The most visible features of the state's spending and taxing policies during the 1980s have been the massive military buildup, the cutbacks in domestic social programs, the shift of the tax burden from capital to labor, and an alarming growth in budget deficits, hence the total national debt and the interest paid on the debt (see Table 6.1).

The data in Table 6.1 reveal that military spending has risen dramatically during the 1980s: while it grew from $90.4 billion in 1970 to $155.2 billion in 1980—an increase of 72 percent—it reached $328.4 billion in 1990, an increase of 112 percent in only a decade. This is clearly evident, especially when one looks at long-term trends in military spending since World War II (see Figure 6.1).

The growth in military spending during the 1980s, writes Victor Perlo, "was a faster pace of increase than occurred during the Vietnam War. . . . In real terms, adjusting for price changes, the Reagan Administration went well beyond the Korean and Vietnam War peaks in weapons procurement" (1988, 306–7). "The 'Star Wars' program initiated in 1983," he points out, has been "the biggest source of profiteering, relatively, of any military program":

> Starting with a $1 billion appropriation in 1984, the amount was scheduled to rise to $7.3 billion in 1989. And this represented only the preliminary stages of what *Time* magazine called "The Star Wars Sweepstakes," [which] . . . "could ultimately cost anywhere from $400 billion to $1.2

Table 6.1
Military Spending, Federal Deficit, and Interest Paid on Debt,
1970–1992 (in billions of current dollars)

Year	Military Spending	Gross Federal Debt	Annual Budget Deficits	Net Interest Paid
1970	90.4	382.6	-2.8	13.5
1971	88.7	409.5	-23.0	14.1
1972	89.9	437.3	-23.4	14.0
1973	88.7	468.4	-14.9	15.7
1974	92.7	486.2	-6.1	19.6
1975	103.1	544.1	-53.2	21.7
1976	108.0	631.9	-73.7	25.1
1977	115.2	709.1	-53.6	28.5
1978	123.5	780.4	-59.2	33.5
1979	136.2	833.8	-40.2	40.7
1980	155.2	914.3	-73.8	50.8
1981	180.5	1,003.9	-78.9	66.7
1982	209.3	1,147.0	-127.9	82.2
1983	234.7	1,381.9	-207.8	90.6
1984	253.0	1,576.7	-185.3	109.7
1985	280.7	1,827.5	-212.3	128.3
1986	292.4	2,130.0	-221.2	136.8
1987	308.8	2,355.3	-150.4	141.7
1988	319.8	2,600.8	-155.1	151.4
1989	333.7	2,866.2	-152.0	171.1
1990	328.4	3,206.3	-220.4	184.2
1991[a]	330.4	3,617.8	-318.1	197.0
1992[a]	328.2	4,021.1	-280.9	206.3

Note: [a]Estimate by the U.S. Office of Management and Budget.

Sources: U.S. Office of Management and Budget, *Historical Tables, Budget of the United States Government, 1987*; U.S. Bureau of the Census, *Statistical Abstract of the United States: 1987*, p. 292; U.S. Council of Economic Advisers, *Economic Report of the President, 1988*, pp. 338-39; *1990*, pp. 383-89; U.S. Office of Management and Budget, *Budget of the United States Government, Fiscal Year 1992*, part 2, pp. 183, 287, and part 4, p. 3.

Figure 6.1
Military Spending, 1947–1991 (in billions of constant 1985 dollars)

Source: Constructed with data from U.S. Bureau of the Census, *Statistical Abstract of the United States* (various years); U.S. Office of Management and Budget, *Budget of the United States Government, Fiscal Year 1992.*

trillion. It would thus become the biggest bonanza ever for American business and educational institutions" (1988, 313).

Pointing to the strong ties between the Pentagon and the military contractors, Perlo goes on to document that

> there is increasing overlapping between the dominant munitions firms and industrial monopolies as a whole. . . . As of the mid-1980s, half of the 100 largest industrial and transport companies were among the 100 largest Pentagon contractors; *while 23 of the top 25 armament contractors were among the 100 largest industrial concerns.*
> Among the 100 largest arms merchants were the foremost corporations manufacturing heavy electrical equipment, electronics, computers, metals, chemicals, petroleum (1988, 313).

The sharp increase in military spending under the Reagan administration in the 1980s, coupled with the granting of huge tax cuts to the wealthy, which resulted in a reduction in government revenues, led to large budget deficits. Thus while the annual federal deficits averaged about $37 billion in the 1970s they averaged $177 billion in the 1980s—a 378 percent increase in average annual deficits over the previous decade (see Table 6.1 and Figure 6.2). While there was a notable decrease in the annual deficits in the last few years of the 1980s—from a high of $221 billion in 1986 down to around $150 billion in subsequent years—the 1990–1991 recession and the cost of the Gulf War in 1991 led to a

Figure 6.2
Annual Federal Deficits, 1960–1992 (in billions of dollars)

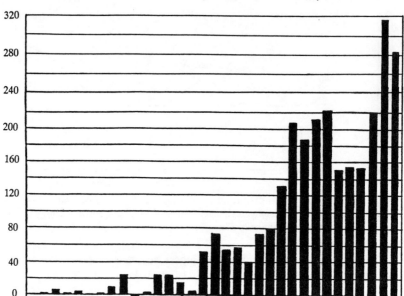

Note: Data for 1991 and 1992 are estimates by the Office of Management and Budget.

Sources: Constructed with data from U.S. Office of Management and Budget, *Historical Tables, Budget of the United States Government, 1987*; U.S. Bureau of the Census, *Statistical Abstract of the United States* (various years); U.S. Council of Economic Advisers, *Economic Report of the President, 1990*; U.S. Office of Management and Budget, *Budget of the United States Government, Fiscal Year 1992*, part 2, p. 287.

sharp increase in the deficit, rising to $220 billion in 1990 and projected to reach $318 billion in 1991 and $281 billion in 1992 (U.S. OMB 1991, Part 2, p. 287).

Likewise, the national debt increased from just above $900 billion in 1980 to over $3 trillion in 1990—triple the 1980 amount in a single decade. With the sharp increase in the deficit projected for 1991–92 and for subsequent years, it is estimated that the total national debt would reach $4 trillion by 1992 (U.S. OMB 1991, Part 2, p. 287). The annual net interest paid on the debt has similarly grown to unprecedented levels: while it amounted to $13.5 billion in 1970 and averaged $23 billion during the 1970s, it reached $50.8 billion in 1980 and continued its growth at triple-digit levels from 1984 on, averaging $113 billion in the 1980s and $140 billion between 1984 and 1990 (see Table 6.1). In 1990, the net interest on the $3.2 trillion debt had reached $184.2 billion (U.S. OMB 1991, Part 4, p. 3).

Total nonfinancial debt, that is, total debt accumulated by government, households, and nonfinancial businesses, reached nearly $10 trillion—an amount equivalent to more than 180 percent of GNP—with the sharpest increase taking place during the 1980s (see Figure 6.3).

All in all, the 1980s was a period of spiraling annual deficits, growing accumulated debt, and rising net interest on the debt—all fueled by an unprecedented growth in peacetime military spending and the biggest probusiness tax cut to large corporations and the wealthiest individuals in the United States in recent decades.

The fiscal crisis of the state, exacerbated by the bonanza for the rich and the blank check for the Pentagon during the 1980s, fell disproportionately on the working class and the poor, who came to shoulder the ever-growing burden of taxation. According to a Congressional Budget Office report released in 1987, low-income families would pay nearly 20 percent higher taxes in 1988 than they did the year before, while the richest 10 percent of families would pay 6–10 percent less in taxes and the wealthiest 1 percent would pay 19–25 percent less (Feagin and Feagin 1990, 59). The Reagan administration's promises of "across-the-board" tax cuts notwithstanding, 95 percent of Americans paid a

Figure 6.3
Nonfinancial Debt as Percentage of GNP, 1950–1989

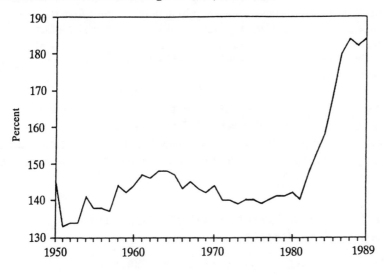

Source: Dollars & Sense, no. 156 (May 1990), p. 23.

greater proportion of their incomes in federal taxes in 1988 than they did a decade earlier. Moreover, while "the wealthiest 1 percent of the families had an average tax cut of $44,750 in 1988, the tax rate for poverty-level families of four [increased] from 1.8 percent of their income in 1979 to 10.8 percent in 1986" (Feagin and Feagin 1990, 59).

Accounting for the greatest share of federal revenues, individual income taxes and social security taxes—the bulk of which are collected from workers for future retirement benefits—have continued to increase over the past several decades: in 1960 individual income taxes and social security taxes together accounted for 59.9 percent of total federal revenues, but by 1970 they had risen to 70.1 percent, by 1980 to 77.8 percent, and by 1989 to 81 percent (U.S. Bureau of the Census 1981, 247; 1990, 310). On the other hand, corporate taxes, which in the mid-1940s accounted for 34 percent of all taxes collected by the federal government, by 1960 had dropped to 20.2 percent, by 1970 to 16.9 percent, by 1980 to 12.4 percent, and by 1989 to 10.97 percent (U.S. Bureau of the Census 1981, 247; 1990, 310).[30] Thus while the proportion of total taxes paid by the working class sharply increased in recent decades,

> a large proportion of the largest companies paid little or no tax in at least one year since the mid-1970s. . . . Forty large corporations that paid no taxes in 1986 . . . [and] at least sixteen large corporations, whose combined profits totaled almost $10 billion in 1987, not only paid *no* taxes, but together received more than $1 billion in tax refunds *from* the federal government in that year. Topping this list were General Motors, with profits of $2.4 billion and a refund of $742.2 million, and IBM, with profits of $2.9 billion and a refund of $123.5 million (Feagin and Feagin 1990, 60–61).

The changes in the proportion of taxes paid by corporations and individuals during the past several decades indicate a shift in the tax burden to finance state expenditures—away from corporations and the wealthy and toward the working class and other sectors of the general population.

THE STATE'S RESPONSE TO THE CRISIS: BUSINESS AS USUAL

As we have seen earlier in this chapter, the state's response to the systemwide crisis of capitalism in the United States in the last two decades has been such that it has further deepened the contradictions of the system. The transfer of wealth from the middle-income working population and the poor to the capitalists, with the stated purpose of stimulating growth and expanding the economy to generate new revenues, has not yielded any positive results in this direction; instead, it has given rise to renewed speculation, mergers and acquisitions, a shift toward short-term quick profits, and accelerated overseas expansion and led to reshuffling of financial assets to accumulate more capital (Perlo 1988).

The widening gap between the acumulated wealth of the capitalist class and the declining incomes of workers (within a deteriorating national economy and the state's fiscal crisis) has led to the ensuing political crisis within the state apparatus over budgetary priorities. The failure of the state in channeling its resources in a direction that promotes reindustrialization and increases employment, incomes, and purchasing power to raise the living standards of the population can only be explained by the lack of serious committment on the part of the state to rescuing the economy (and the state itself) from the socioeconomic crisis that has affected, and continues to affect, adversely a substantial segment of the laboring people in the United States. This has been the case because the forces controlling the U.S. state—that is, big-business capitalist interests—have sought to advance solely their own exclusive class interests, despite the negative impact of these on the economy and society in general, as well as the state.[31]

This was precisely the nature of President Bush's supply-side-oriented capital-gains tax cut proposal of 1989:

> Only in a supply-side world would a President propose a tax cut in order to increase government revenues. And only in trickle-down America would this President herald the cut as "tax reform" when 64% of the benefits are targeted to the richest 0.7% of taxpayers, while the bottom 60% of taxpayers would receive less than 3% of the largess. Yet this is precisely what George Bush is proposing with his capital-gains tax cut plan. . . .
>
> A capital-gains tax break would so overwhelmingly benefit the wealthy that it would make the Reagan tax cuts of the early 1980s seem progressive by comparison (Miller 1989, 15).

Going beyond the Reagan tax cuts of 1981, Bush's proposed capital-gains tax cuts were another attempt by the capitalist state to transfer more wealth to the rich, as the wealthiest 5 percent of all taxpayers were slated to receive 85 percent of capital gains. As Miller points out,

Five of every six taxpayers with incomes of more than $1 million a year have capital-gains income, but fewer than one in every 20 taxpayers earning $10,000 or less have it. . . .

For the 80% of families earning less than $60,000 a year the average tax savings from the Bush plan would be only $20 (1989, 17).

After much pressure from progressive groups over several months, the proposed plan was defeated in Congress in 1990, but in the wake of Bush's popularity stemming from the Gulf War he has made further attempts to have Congress pass a similar plan to reward the wealthy, regardless of the devastating consequences of this on the federal budget in the aftermath of the $500 billion savings and loan bailout and the tens of billions of dollars spent on the Gulf War.[32]

It is in this broader context of the state's overextension that the fiscal crisis of the state must be seen and the purpose and direction of state policies understood, for the policies that the state adopts in line with big-business interests may in fact be detrimental to the needs and priorities of American society as a whole and thus have a differential, negative impact on the people, with serious political implications.

Inaction or indifference by the state in solving some of the pressing social problems on the one hand and its openly probusiness positions and policies on the other can in effect be identified as quite in line with the interests of capital and the capitalist class, hence prolonging the prevailing social, economic, and political crisis and preserving the status quo through policies that continue business as usual. Though one cannot expect anything more or different from a state controlled by the capitalist class, its actions in this narrow, limited frame may indeed clash with the interests of the broad segments of the population in general, and the working people in particular, prompting an altogether different response from labor and its rank and file.

We examine this and other related questions concerning the labor movement and its response to the crisis in the next chapter.

Chapter 7

Labor's Response to Economic Decline and Decay

The response of the working class to the deteriorating economic situation in the United States during the past two decades has been a mixed one, with institutional compliance and defeatism at the upper rungs of the traditional labor union bureaucracy on the one hand and increasing rank-and-file militancy and struggle from below across many industries on the other. In the absence of a strong working class movement organized around and led by a radical, labor, socialist, or communist party active among workers—as in France, Italy, Spain, Portugal, Britain, the Scandinavian countries, and much of the rest of Europe and other advanced capitalist countries—workers in the United States have been unable to press for their demands beyond narrowly defined reformist trade union policies of the dominant labor organizations, such as the AFL-CIO.

To be able to more accurately assess labor's overall response to the economic and social crisis of contemporary U.S. capitalism, we will in this chapter examine this response at three levels: (1) the level of the established labor union bureaucracy of organized labor; (2) the level of rank-and-file worker struggles, through strikes, walkouts, protests, and other forms of collective defiance; and (3) the level of party organization and political action by struggles in opposition to the capitalist system that would advance the class struggle.

THE CRISIS OF ORGANIZED LABOR AND THE TRADE UNION BUREAUCRACY

Much of the problem facing labor in the United States today is seen as the result of the crisis of organized labor due in part to the class-collaborationist policies of the national trade union bureaucracy. Whether it be the AFL-CIO, the United Auto Workers (UAW), the Teamsters, or most other major national unions—except some progressive, democratic unions like the United Electrical, Radio and Machine Workers of America (UE) and the International Longshoremen's and Warehousemen's Union (ILWU) (see De Caux 1974; Larrowe 1972)— the bureaucratic leadership of these unions has compromised labor's independent, progressive role by its "partnership" with management (Kimeldorf 1988). Herein lie "the roots of today's labor crisis," according to Gil Green: "As in the twenties, labor leaders no longer see capital as the enemy and, as in the twenties, internal crisis is the inevitable consequence. The policies of leadership collide with the essential class nature and purpose of the movement" (1976, 120). Referring to this "class partnership," Green writes: "So insidious and pervasive has this tendency become that even many labor leaders who think they are free of it, in fact, are influenced by and bow to it" (1976, 120). Procapitalist, anticommunist, corrupt union "leaders" such as Gus Tyler of the International Ladies Garment Workers Union (ILGWU), Walter Reuther of the UAW, George Meany of the AFL-CIO, Tony Boyle of the United Mine Workers of America (UMWA), Joe Curran of the National Maritime Union (NMU), and Jimmy Hoffa and Frank Fitzsimmons of the Teamsters Union, to name only a few, were in the forefront of the reactionary, collaborationist process that led to the crisis of organized labor (Hall 1972).[33]

Take, for example, the case of Walter Reuther, president of the UAW, and George Meany, president of the AFL-CIO. Green writes:

In 1966, when his brother Victor charged the AFL-CIO under Meany with being a CIA conduit, funneling money to Latin America to counter Communist influence in unions, columnist Thomas W. Braden disclosed that he had turned over $50,000 to Walter Reuther in behalf of the CIA. Walter Reuther acknowledged receiving the money, but characteristically copped a plea. It was an "emergency situation," he said, because the "weak European labor unions" were especially "vulnerable to Communist subversion."

The difference between Meany and Reuther boiled down to this: Reuther was ready to do the bidding of the CIA in "emergency" situations, while Meany believed the "emergency" was permanent. Neither saw anything wrong in subverting labor unions in other countries in the interests of American capital (1976, 123).

At home, Reuther was equally insensitive to the needs and demands of labor, least of all to labor's rank-and-file, minority, women, and young workers, and to the democratic impulses of the workers on the shop floor.

Charges of corruption, the influence of organized crime, and collaboration with corporate and governmental institutions, such as the CIA, were not simply directed at the Teamsters and the AFL-CIO leadership. Many of the major national unions during the 1960s and the 1970s came under similar criticism from labor's rank and file (Morris 1971). As a result,

the hierarchical, centralized bureaucracy of the national unions became more isolated from the rank and file. Because of this insulation, the national union leadership frequently misjudged the desires of the membership and recommended contracts which the rank and file turned down. This became a frequent occurrence in the 1960s and 1970s (Nissen 1981, 24).

The resurgence of rank-and-file militancy from below through the struggles of the coal miners within the UMWA who succeeded in throwing out the corrupt Boyle leadership, the grassroots campaigns of the Teamsters' rank and file through the formation of Teamsters for a Democratic Union (TDU), the similar efforts of rank-and-file steelworkers led by Ed Sadlowski, and the progressive steps taken by the machinists' union led by William Winpisinger did play an important role in activating the labor movement in the 1970s and 1980s, but could not reverse the decline of organized labor and rescue the labor movement from its current crisis. Thus continued the reign of the conservative union officialdom throughout this period—a period of give-backs, concessions, and a generalized assault on the working class and the labor movement.[34]

Under the headline "American Labor's Worst Decade since the 1920's," labor activist and executive director of the Labor Education and Research Project Kim Moody writes:

The 1980s were the worst decade American labor has experienced since the 1920s. Global and domestic economic forces long in the making were harnessed to a government-encouraged corporate drive to redistribute income in favor of business. This employers' offensive went beyond aggressive bargaining to include union-busting, scab-herding, new modes of technological and psychological control, and the sweeping reorganization of workplaces from smokestack plants to digitally-driven offices.

Seemingly helpless before such forces, U.S. labor officials presided over the proliferation of contract concessions, the demise of industry-wide and pattern contracts, and, in some cases, even the surrender of the union's role as defender of the distinct interests of the workers (1990, 7).

The conservative promanagement top union officials—in point of fact, the entire upper crust of the collaborationist labor hierarchy—were interested more in the maintenance of the status quo through the signing of sellout labor contracts than in guiding the workers in their struggle against the bosses, let alone the capitalist system itself.

Faced by a mounting corporate attack on labor in the aftermath of the crushing defeat the Professional Air Traffic Controllers Association (PATCO) suffered in the early years of the Reagan administration at the beginning of the 1980s, the union officialdom remained helpless against the bosses' offensive to lower labor costs and increase profits.

This set the stage for a protracted attack on labor by capital, sanctioned by the capitalist state. Writing about these developments in the early 1980s, Bruce Nissen stated:

Aggressive union-busting, decertification campaigns, hard-line bargaining aimed at cutting real wages, relocating plants to non-union environments, and a whole host of conservative and reactionary legislative initiatives are some of the signs of what is now going on (1981, 26).

The corporate offensive included the acceleration of the move to nonunion, low-wage regions of the country and to cheap-labor areas overseas where direct investments were supplemented by subcontracting arrangements and out-sourcing schemes, conversion of full-time work into part-time work that would keep unions away and reduce costs in paid-out benefits, filing for bankruptcy to "reorganize" companies and thereby to get rid of the union, the establishment of two-tiered wage scales that pay much less to newly hired workers for doing the same work, as well as demanding rollbacks, give-backs, wage and benefit reductions, and other concessions from the unions (Harrison and Bluestone 1988).

All these have led to a steady decline in wages, as more and more unions have followed suit in accepting wage cuts or freezes throughout the 1980s:

The dramatic drop in average wage increases beginning in 1982 came as more and more workers took wage cuts or freezes. In 1983 contracts, 37%

of private, non-farm workers and 56% of manufacturing workers took freezes or cuts. For manufacturing workers the worst year was 1986 when 60% took freezes or cuts.

In 1989, the seventh year of recovery, 10% of all workers and 17% of manufacturing workers with new contracts took freezes or cuts (Moody 1990, 8).

This was matched by cuts in benefits in health care, pensions, and other forms of compensation. "After their success in flattening out wages," Moody continues, "employers have turned toward cuts in benefits":

Health plans have been a major target as employers attempt to shift premium payments to workers and move to cheaper plans. The percentage of workers with fully-paid health plans fell from 72% in 1980 to 45% in 1986.

Not surprisingly, payroll deductions for health plans have increased throughout the decade. The Service Employees International Union (SEIU) estimates that employee payroll deductions in 178 SEIU-negotiated plans rose 56% in the past two years [1988–1990] alone (1990, 9).

Declining wages, reduction or loss of benefits, and a general deterioration in the position of organized labor, effected by a number of additional factors that are discussed below, have made unions less attractive to new nonunion workers, thus contributing to the proportionate decline in union membership relative to the growing labor force—a development that has now reached crisis proportions.

The decline in union membership during recent decades has its roots in more fundamental structural changes in the U.S. political economy that have been taking place with increasing speed during the postwar period.[35] These are: (1) increasing automation and computerization of the production process, requiring fewer workers and the replacement of a growing segment of the work force by sophisticated machinery and technology; (2) the internationalization of capital and the production process and the relocation of factories to cheap-labor areas overseas, resulting in plant closings in the United States, thus leading to loss of jobs for millions of unionized workers; (3) a shift in the U.S. economy from industrial production to the service sector, the sector that is the least organized and pays the lowest wages; and (4) the growth and success of anti-union activities by private firms, coupled with the weakening and weak enforcement of existing labor legislation, especially during the right-wing Reagan administration in the 1980s. These four factors, together with historical forces that have stifled the growth and development of the labor movement, have been the key contributing causes of the decline in union membership and the weakening of the labor movement in recent decades (Lembcke 1988).

Thus while in 1945 35 percent of the nonagricultural labor force was organized, by 1970 it had declined to 31 percent, by 1979 to 25 percent, and by 1988 to 14 percent (U.S. Bureau of the Census 1990, 419). A comparison of unionization level of 16 advanced capitalist countries shows that, in 1985, the United States had by far the least unionized work force in the advanced capitalist world (see Table 7.1).[36] Moreover, in 1988, while only 14 percent of the U.S. work force was unionized, a mere 6 percent of service workers and 6.7 percent of workers in wholesale and retail trade were union members, while the rate for younger workers ages 16–24 was 6.2 percent (U.S. Bureau of the Census 1990, 419).

Despite these difficulties and the unresponsive leadership of the dominant national unions during the course of the past few decades, workers in many industries across the country have waged important struggles through strikes, walkouts, protests, and other forms of defiance to put the bosses on notice that they could no longer take the workers for granted and expect the complacency and defeatism fostered by the national union bureaucracy that serve corporate schemes of labor control. The victories achieved in rank-and-file struggles of the 1970s and 1980s are, if anything, a testimony to the fact that there is a way out of labor's crisis—one that requires a much more resilient nationwide effort to unleash rank-and-file militancy on an unprecedented scale since the 1930s, so that the 1990s (as were the 1930s) would once again become a decade of militant labor struggles at the grass roots level.

RANK-AND-FILE STRUGGLES

Throughout the 1970s and 1980s workers in many industries across the United States engaged in a large number of strikes, walkouts, and other forms of protest against their employers, often despite the directives of their unions advising them not to engage in such actions. Many of the rank-and-file struggles were in fact for the very right to strike, which the bosses tried to take away through hastily drawn union contracts agreed to by the tacitly compliant national union bureaucracies, as in the case of the coal miners' strikes in the early and late 1970s. A key weapon of workers to express their grievances against their employers, the right to strike was seen by many workers as an inalienable right of collective

Table 7.1

Level of Unionization in 16 Advanced Capitalist Countries, 1970–1985 (in percent)

Country	Level of Unionization			Change in Level of Unionization		
	1970	1979	1985	1970-1979	1979-1985	1970-1985
Denmark	66	86	98	20	12	32
Finland	56	84	85	28	1	29
Sweden	79	89	95	10	6	16
Ireland	44	49	51	5	2	7
Italy	39	51	45	12	-6	6
France	22	28	28	6	0	6
Australia	52	58	57	6	-1	5
Germany	37	42	42	5	0	5
Canada	32	36	37	4	1	5
Switzerland	31	36	35	5	-1	4
Norway	59	60	61	1	1	2
United Kingdom	51	58	52	7	-6	1
Netherlands	39	43	37	4	-6	-2
Austria	64	59	61	-5	2	-3
Japan	35	32	29	-3	-3	-6
United States	31	25	18	-6	-7	-13

Source: Richard Freeman, "Contraction and Expansion: The Divergence of Private Sector and Public Sector Unionism in the United States," *Journal of Economic Perspectives* 2, no. 2 (Spring 1988), cited in *Dollars & Sense*, no. 139 (September 1988), p. 22.

expression, and none were willing to sign any contract that would deny them this basic right.[37]

The period from the late 1970s on saw intensified rank-and-file struggles in confronting the power of capital at the point of production. More and more workers began to take the initiative on the rungs below to exert their collective strength and fight back to protect their benefits and rights (Fantasia 1988).

In 1978, some five years after the earlier uproar in "bloody Harlan County," more than 160,000 coal miners belonging to the UMWA again went on strike, which lasted several months, ending only when the government intervened with the full force of the Taft-Hartley Act.

In 1979 over 35,000 International Harvester workers walked off their jobs, striking the company for five and a half months. Throughout the 170 days of the strike the workers held firm across the country, keeping the company shut down during the winter months. Faced with estimated losses of as much as $500 million, the company surrendered.

In early 1980 more than 60,000 U.S. and Canadian oil and petrochemical workers, members of the Oil, Chemical and Atomic Workers Union (OCAW), went on strike against the giant fuel monopolies, such as Gulf, Texaco, and Cities Service, while more than 1,000 angry steelworkers, protesting U.S. Steel's plan to shut down its Ohio and McDonald Steelworks, took over the Youngstown headquarters of the giant steel corporation and demanded that their jobs be saved.

The turn of events in the early 1980s, with the inauguration of the right-wing Reagan administration, posed another challenge to labor when the firing of some 11,000 striking air traffic controllers—members of PATCO—in 1981 marked the beginning of the attack on labor that was later to force other workers to make concessions by taking wage cuts and a reduction in their hard-won benefits that they had fought for during the previous decade. This did not mean, however, that labor struggles came to an end.

In March 1981, for example, 170,000 miners belonging to the UMWA went on strike once again. In June, unions representing more than 500,000 postal workers demonstrated in a National Postal Action Day, demanding a contract providing safe working conditions, a shorter workweek, higher wages, and an improved cost-of-living clause, among other benefits.

In September 1981, upwards of 400,000 workers gathered in Washington, D.C., on Solidarity Day, one of the largest protest demonstrations in U.S. history. Tens of thousands of workers also demonstrated in other cities throughout the country, bringing the total to well over half a million.

In a report to the 350 convention delegates at the national convention of the UE union in September 1981, the union's three top officers condemned Reaganomics in these terms: "Put simply, the Reagan economic plan involves an enormous transfer of the wealth of the country from the working people and the poor to the super rich and their corporations" (quoted in Spektor 1981, 4).

In March 1982 more than 30,000 demonstrators marched in New York City against Reagan administration policies. Among the protesters were trade unionists, unemployed workers, students, church groups, veterans, and other progressive sectors of society. Speaker after speaker denounced Reagan domestic and foreign policies. In October over 23,000 Caterpillar workers went out on strike after the company refused to budge from its insistence on 76 concessions in a new contract with the UAW.

The deep recession of 1982 made the situation of workers that much worse, as the immediate concern among workers became one of protecting jobs. The 10 percent official unemployment rate, which forced the ranks of the unemployed to swell to over 11 million, with millions more unemployed and underemployed unaccounted for by the official statistics, placed the workers on the defensive and forced on them more concessions, thus pressing real incomes of workers in a downward direction, as we have documented in previous chapters. Despite these difficulties, however, workers continued to fight back through sustained strike action.

In July 1983 some 3,000 copper miners in Arizona went out on strike against the Phelps Dodge company. In one of the longest strikes in U.S. labor history, lasting over a year, the copper miners stood firm to protect their union rights.

In August 1983 more than 700,000 workers went out on strike against what was at the time the world's biggest monopoly, American Telephone & Telegraph (AT&T). Demanding job security, decent wages, medical care, and an end to discrimination, the hundreds of thousands of striking telephone workers paralyzed the phone system nationwide. Just one week after the AT&T strike, 40,000 Western Electric workers walked out in support of the striking AT&T workers on the picket lines.

In April 1985 over 150,000 people marched nationwide for jobs, peace, and justice. Organized labor, youth, minorities, and other progressive voices were heard in a number of cities across the nation. In Washington, D.C., 75,000 gathered; in San Francisco, 50,000; in Seattle, Houston, Denver, and Los Angeles, 30,000.

In July 1986 over 15,000 city workers, members of the American Federation of State, County and Municipal Employees (AFSCME) went on strike in Philadelphia to save their jobs and health benefits.

In October 1986 nearly 30,000 members of the International Longshoremen's Association went on strike in ports from Maine to Virginia along the eastern coastline of the United States.

In April 1987 more than 45,000 workers representing the labor movement took part in an antiwar march of 150,000 in Washington, D.C. Protesting against U.S. intervention in Central America, the workers also demanded that plant closings and layoffs be stopped, as well as unemployment, racism, and the rollback in wages and benefits.

In May 1987 thousands of meatpacking workers, members of United Food and Commercial Workers, went on strike at the John Morrell meatpacking plant in Sioux Falls, South Dakota. Later, in August, several thousand trade unionists and their supporters from the Great Plains states converged on the city in a militant demonstration of support for the striking workers.

In January 1988 all commercial shipping in every port in Oregon and Washington came to a standstill as 3,500 Northwest longshore workers went out on strike in ports along more than 400 miles of coastline from Bellingham, Washington, to Coos Bay, Oregon.

In March 1989 more than 8,000 members of the International Association of Machinists (IAM) went on strike against Eastern Airlines, which turned into one of the longest strikes in U.S. history.

In April 1989 thousands of Pittston miners in Virginia went on strike and stood firm in their stand against the coal companies, despite widespread intimidation and the force of the state police and the courts unleashed against them.

These and other, more recent developments in rank-and-file struggles at the close of the 1980s have led some labor analysts to express a sense of optimism in the prospects for labor in the 1990s: "In the last years of the eighties," writes Jane Slaughter of *Labor Notes*, "it has seemed that more and more unionists have been willing to strike or take other dramatic action against their employers":

> The Mine Workers called it "class warfare" in southwest Virginia as they battled the Pittston Coal Co., state police, and the courts.
>
> Hundreds of union supporters in International Falls, Minnesota, routed scab construction workers by storming their camp and burning their trailers.
>
> From Eastern Airlines to NYNEX, from contract rejections in the Teamsters to Southern organizing wins by the Amalgamated Clothing Workers, the militancy has caused some in the labor movement to speak hopefully of "an upsurge," even "a turning point."
>
> Many of these struggles received an impressive showing of solidarity from other unionists (1990, 7).

In many unions across the country the late 1980s was also a period of greater rank-and-file demands for union democracy and control—demands provoked by dissatisfaction with the policies of the top union leadership. These developments include

the New Directions Movement in the United Auto Workers, Ron Carey's campaign for the presidency of the Teamsters, the election of Tony Mazzocchi as secretary-treasurer of the Oil, Chemical and Atomic Workers, and a new Black leadership in the Mail Handlers Union, formerly under the control of racist and mob-dominated officials (Slaughter 1990, 7).

This "upsurge" in rank-and-file activism, Slaughter notes, "is better described as the intensifying of a trend in the labor movement, a trend which is slowly growing and, just as important, which is slowly becoming more conscious of itself" (1990, 8).

CLASS CONSCIOUSNESS, CLASS STRUGGLE, AND THE ROLE OF A WORKERS' PARTY

The development of class consciousness among the working class is not an automatic process, but it is nonetheless a direct outcome of the conditions of work and life under capitalism experienced by millions of workers (Lembcke 1988). This process, once fully developed, draws workers into the class struggle—a struggle that is political in nature and is waged against the ruling capitalist class and the entire institutional structure of the capitalist system, including the state (Berberoglu 1990).

Historically, the central facilitators of the development of class consciousness and class struggle, beyond the narrow economic battles waged through the instrumentality of trade unions at the point of production, have been workers' political associations and parties—that is, organizations of workers that have articulated and advanced the class interests of the working class in a broader political context, with the aim of taking state power away from the capitalists.

The longer history of capitalist development in Europe led at an earlier period to the development of radical workers' organizations of different political persuasions—from anarcho-syndicalist to communist, as well as traditional reformist—as manifested in the Paris Commune, the First International, and later the Bolsheviks, among others. Various radical anarcho-syndicalist, socialist, communist, and other labor organizations and parties thus have their origins in these and other struggles of the working class against capitalism in Europe from the late eighteenth to the early twentieth century (see Katznelson and Zolberg 1986).

In the United States, the later development of capitalism delayed by a century the emergence of a broad-based workers' struggle against it but did result in the formation of similar, parallel organizations informed by these collective historic experiences of labor that span over two centuries. By the mid nineteenth century, the U.S. working class had all the signs of a maturing proletariat ready to take on the system that controlled and exploited them so brutally (Boyer and Morais 1980). Playing a critical role in the Civil War and in the victory over the slave system that blocked the further development of its interests in the fight against capitalism in the North, the U.S. working class scored many victories in determined struggles against the bosses that were often bloody and caused labor some tragic setbacks, to be sure.[38] But the momentum of these struggles in the late nineteenth century resulted in the formation and development of important labor organizations in this period and well into the early twentieth century: the Knights of Labor, the Industrial Workers of the World, the Socialist party, the Communist party, and numerous other politically oriented radical unions and parties were all the outcome of this unfolding process of maturing working-class consciousness and class struggle that labor began to wage during this period of turmoil and unrest in the United States (Boyer and Morais 1980).

Similar struggles during the Great Depression, led by the Communist party, scored important victories in organizing efforts through unions and political action, for example, through the CIO, to improve the condition of labor, while at the same time helping to advance working-class consciousness among a growing number of workers who had found themselves in the midst of a great economic catastrophe of rarely seen proportions (Green 1976, 27–51; Stepan-Norris and Zeitlin 1989). As Gil Green writes,

> What made the difference in the thirties was not only the greater depth of economic and social crisis, but the preparatory work before the conditions of upsurge had fully matured in order to bring them to fruition. The Communists and other left-wing militants slowly and methodically began to organize. . . . By their example they proved that organization was possible, and by their policies they helped bring about the necessary unity (1976, 178–79).

The postwar repression of labor, which through the McCarthyist witch-hunts and expulsions of leftists from the major unions, such as the

CIO and the UAW (see Keeran 1980; Levenstein 1981), effectively set back the labor movement by many years, had a devastating impact on labor's political muscle, for it neutralized the influence of organized leftist groups on the labor movement and the direction it took in the conservative 1950s—a predicament from which U.S. labor was never able to recover to this day.[39]

The class-collaborationist leadership and policies of the sanitized postwar AFL-CIO officialdom that, in the absence of a strong socialist or communist presence, came to define the nature of "business unionism" wedded to reformist capitalist party politics rallied behind the Democratic party is what distinguishes the current state of the U.S. labor movement from its counterparts in Europe and elsewhere in the advanced capitalist world. The decisive current presence and role of communist, socialist, labor, and other workers' political parties in Europe (and their absence or extreme weakness in the United States) is the chief factor that explains the differential position and prospects of labor in Europe and the United States in recent decades. The existence and strength of an independent workers' political party is, therefore, of crucial importance to labor and the labor movement in its political (class) struggle against the capitalist state.

Things are beginning to change on this front, however. There are renewed calls for the establishment of a new, independent workers' party, while other existing older parties and organizations on the left are beginning to mobilize their forces and energies with increasing vigor.[40] As the transformation of the world economy continues and the internationalization of U.S. capital further weakens the U.S. domestic economy and plunges it into a depressionary crisis in the coming years in sectors of the economy in which organized labor has heretofore been concentrated and, as a result of this, U.S. workers begin to experience a further decline in their standard of living, there will be increasing pressure from below to mobilize and fight back to regain the resilience and power labor once had and exercised in order to advance its own interests. The critical factor in this regard will increasingly become the central role of an independent workers' party that will have to take up the task of leading U.S. labor in the class struggle that will surely intensify and spread in the years ahead.

Chapter 8

Conclusion: Which Way out of the Crisis?

We have shown throughout this book that the United States has entered, during the course of the past two decades, a period of irreversible economic decline that has fueled a number of social and political, as well as economic, problems. The most important of these has been increasing class polarization as manifested in the widening gap between capital and labor, with its race and gender dimensions. That this decline, relative to other centers of global capitalism, and its consequent contradictions stemming from the accelerated internationalization of U.S. capital is a central legacy of the U.S. empire is hardly disputed by serious observers of the U.S. political economy over the past several decades. That legacy, however, is the result of a contradictory process: while the living standard of an increasing number of workers has declined, the position of the wealthy owners of transnational corporations has greatly expanded, leading to greater concentration of wealth and income, hence further centralization of capital.

In the period following World War II, the United States emerged as the leading center of the capitalist world economy and soon positioned itself as the sole superpower, controlling the economic lifeline of the global industrial and financial system established by earlier imperial powers. During this period, the U.S. state played a central supportive role in the expansion of capital and in laying down the foundations of U.S. global hegemony throughout the capitalist world. As a result, U.S. capital experienced an unprecedented expansion of its economic power on a world scale and gradually came to dominate the economies of Europe, the Pacific Rim, and the Third World, which went unchallenged until recently. With this economic power came political and military power when the U.S. state became the global protector of the interests of U.S. transnational capital and thereby came to take up its central role as an imperial state whose reach extended to every corner of the capitalist world.

By the early 1970s, the contradictions embedded in this process of global economic and political domination reached its peak, such that, coupled with the U.S. defeat in Vietnam and the resurgence of anti-imperialist national liberation struggles on the one hand and the rise of the European and Japanese economies and their reemergence on the world scene on the other, U.S. hegemony over the global capitalist system came under serious challenge.

On the domestic front, as the U.S. monopolies reached their height and expanded beyond their national boundaries on a grand scale throughout the postwar period, the consequent internationalization of the production process resulted in the contraction of the U.S. industrial base, such that access to cheap labor abroad meant growing unemployment at home, which, in turn, reduced the aggregate purchasing power of the American worker, thus ironically putting into jeopardy the profitability of U.S. transnationals in the form of a realization crisis—for how could the products produced cheaply abroad be sold to an increasingly unemployed or underemployed work force in the United States affected by the internationalization process that has so negatively impacted the key industrial sectors of the U.S. domestic economy? Herein lie the broader contradictions of the system, that is, between its global interests in capital accumulation (hence profitability on a world scale) and its domestic consequences, both for labor and the economy as a whole.

It is in this context that the state has come in to play its role in facilitating the capital accumulation process through liberal (Keynesian) or conservative (supply-side) policies, depending on the particular administration representing one or another fraction of the capitalist class. While the postwar Keynesian policies of the U.S. state have generally been aimed at stabilizing the economy through increased public spending to regulate and control the domestic consequences of the internationalization of U.S. capital, a shift in these policies during the conservative 1980s has signaled the emergence in centers of political power of the most reactionary sectors of U.S. capital accommodated within the framework of overall control of the U.S. state by the monopoly sector. The shift in government policy in a rightist direction in both the economy and the polity is thus a result of the emergence of these new forces, operating in a way that advances the interests of the monopoly sector in this most desperate phase of U.S. global and domestic economic decline, which has lent itself to increased militarization and global interventionism. This has been accompanied with the wholesale transfer of wealth from labor to capital, from the poor to the rich, as manifested in tax cuts for the wealthy, reduced funding of social programs, increased military spending, and huge budget deficits resulting from these, while necessitating the payment of ever-larger interest on the growing national debt. All these and other related policies of the monopoly-controlled state have led to the deterioration of the domestic economy and effected a decline in the living standards of the working class in the United States, which we have documented at length in this book.

While capital's response to the decline and decay of the U.S. economy has been further concentration and centralization of wealth in a few hands through mergers, acquisitions, takeovers, and buyouts, yielding greater profits and enlarging the assets of the wealthy owners of U.S.-based transnational monopolies, and the state's response to the crisis has been the continuation of the same failed probusiness policies favoring the rich in the midst of a declining national economy and a bankrupt national treasury, labor and progressive forces on the side of the working class have been the only reasoned voices advocating salvaging the remaining pieces of the shattered economy before the impending collapse of the capitalist system gives way to a 1930s-style total economic catastrophe.

So far, the organized labor movement has not, however, taken the initiative to launch an all-out offensive to halt capital's assault on organized labor and the working class in general. And this has reduced morale among workers and given rise to a variety of right-wing racist groups capitalizing on workers' feelings of resentment and outrage against capital and the capitalist state, misdirecting their anger away from the capitalists and the state and toward racial and ethnic minorities or foreigners, most of whom are workers themselves. The absence of an organized and coordinated labor offensive has provided a blank check for proto-fascist elements within the monopoly capitalist class and to its "neo-populist" right-wing shock troops to set the stage for the next round of the crisis threatening the very existence of a declining empire in retreat, a military solution as a way out of the social and economic crisis—one that entails increased military interventionism abroad and political repression and control at home.

There are, however, growing signs of a new rank-and-file insurgency within the labor movement and an expanding multiracial/multinational working-class coalition that is beginning to link up with other progressive forces in society to confront the rapidly deteriorating conditions affecting a growing number of working people. As the crisis worsens and more workers become affected by a further deterioration of the economy, they will in turn contribute to the growth of a new coalition of forces that will increasingly come to challenge the capitalist class and the capitalist state, in effect the very foundations of capitalist society.

Such conditions have in the past led to civil wars and revolutions, and nothing in the American experience precludes or prevents just such an outcome if events warrant it and the underlying material conditions lead to it. The only missing factors in this formula for change and social transformation of systemic proportions remain class consciousness and its corollary, political organization. Although these are not processes that develop automatically—in fact, it requires a great deal of effort to attain them—the material conditions that would set the stage for the working class to accomplish the necessary tasks to defend itself and advance its class interests are well in place and are developing with increasing speed. To bring these goals to their fruition, it now remains for the highly class-conscious and dedicated workers and their allies to provide the necessary leadership to set the great masses of the working class into motion—a movement that, in the final analysis, represents the only viable way out of the crisis of capitalist society that afflicts the United States today.

Notes

1. The argument of the negative impact of excessive military spending on the economy is certainly not a new one. A similar argument was made earlier by Seymour Melman, in the 1960s (see Melman 1965). For an elaboration of this theme, in the context of the growing relationship between the economy and the military establishment, see Melman 1970.

2. Thus "the rise and fall of empires" in this context can be seen as nothing other than the rise and fall of capitalist classes of rival economic powers across the world. Political-military overextension, therefore, can be seen in this context as an outcome of the underlying economic struggles among competing capitalist classes at the global level. Interimperialist rivalry is thus based not on political or military power and supremacy per se, but on economic strength among rival propertied classes to possess the greatest share of economic wealth in the world. It is only within this economic context that political and military power must be situated. For, as Kennedy would agree, it is the states with the strongest economies incurring the least amount of military expenditure and force (e.g., Germany and Japan today) that would win out in the global struggle for empire status.

3. Going a step further, James Petras correctly observes that "without a clear notion of the antagonistic class interests located in the interior of a social formation, there is a tendency among world system theorists to dissolve the issue into a series of abstract developmental imperatives deduced from a static global stratification system which increasingly resembles the functional requisites and equilibrium models of Parsonian sociology" (1978, 37).

4. The Marshall Plan, proposed by then secretary of state Gen. George Marshall in June 1947, was implemented the following year as the European

Recovery Program. In its four years of operation, the program gave $13 billion to 18 Western European nations (including Greece and Turkey) for a broad variety of investment projects. Over 70 percent of the amount was spent for American goods (Dowd 1977, 235).

5. NATO was established in 1949 as the military counterpart of the Marshall Plan.

6. The relationship between monopolization based on asset size and the domination of markets and a tendency for profits to rise has been shown widely in a number of studies. One such study, conducted at Harvard University in the 1970s, which covered 57 corporations involved in 620 separate businesses, found that the greater the share of the market for a given product that a company monopolized, the higher its rate of profit. Thus, according to the findings of this study, companies controlling less than 7 percent of the market share reported a 9.6 percent return on investment, while those controlling 22–36 percent of the market reported a 17.9 percent return and companies controlling over 36 percent of the market showed a 30.2 percent profit (Cappo 1977, 28).

7. Although economic rivalry between the major capitalist powers has intensified in recent years and surfaced as a major challenge to postwar U.S. hegemony over the world economy, the origins of such rivalry go back nearly a century, to when Britain, France, Germany, Japan, and the United States became part of the worldwide struggle for global supremacy—as manifested, for example, in the struggle over the control of oil in the Middle East at the turn of the century—which later led to World War I.

8. The political implications of this shift away from raw materials investments and toward manufacturing investments are discussed at length in my forthcoming volume on the political economy of development in the Third World (1992, Chapter 3).

9. Nevertheless, in the 1970s and 1980s a growing number of Japanese corporations have been able to move part of their operations into the United States to supply the U.S. market from within, thus avoiding tariffs and other protectionist measures directed against them. Operating, in effect, as "American" corporations, some Japanese firms have thus escaped the problems associated with imports into the United States of goods manufactured abroad. The decline in U.S. wages relative to their increase in Japan during the past decade has been another important incentive for some Japanese firms to move part of their operations into the United States.

10. For an extended discussion on this in a number of Third World countries, see Berberoglu 1992.

11. This, coupled with the possible long-term integration of Eastern Europe into the EEC, may indeed turn Europe into a rival economic superpower in this decade—one that has important political implications.

12. It may be correct to argue that, while the massive 508-point drop in the stock market on "Black Monday" in October 1987 was a reflection of the long-term structural defects in the financial system and the economy in

general, it may in fact prove to be the first concrete sign of a much worse decline to come in the 1990s. An important indicator of continued financial instability in the United States in recent years is the growing number of bank failures, which increased from 11 in 1980, to 80 in 1984, to 221 in 1988. In addition, those identified by the Census Bureau as "problem banks" have grown in number from 217 in 1980, to 848 in 1984, to 1,406 in 1988 (U.S. Bureau of the Census 1990, 497).

13. In 1988 there were 3,487 mergers and acquisitions, totaling $227 billion, up from $53 billion in 1983 (U.S. Bureau of the Census, 1990, 534).

14. It is now estimated that nearly 40 percent of all imports entering the United States are goods produced by overseas subsidiaries of U.S. transnational corporations. In addition, a substantial part of the remainder are produced through subcontracting arrangements between U.S. transnationals and local firms—goods produced in accordance with U.S. corporate specifications for sale at major U.S. retail outlets.

15. In contrast with this, the inflation rate in the 1960s (a period of enormous war profits from the continuing war in Vietnam) was extremely low—about 1 percent per year in the early 1960s and 3 percent per year in the late 1960s (U.S. Bureau of the Census 1987, 455).

16. Except for 1980 and 1981, when the rate was 13.5 percent and 10.4 percent respectively, annual increases in the inflation rate averaged between 3 and 4 percent during the rest of the 1980s, ranging from a low of 1.9 percent in 1986 to a high of 6.1 percent in 1982 (see Table 4.5).

17. It should also be noted that actual gross profits of corporations are often understated, through such practices as intrafirm trade and transfer pricing, in order to reduce tax liabilities across national boundaries. Thus the ratio of gross profits to net profits for many of the largest U.S. transnational corporations may well be higher than can be calculated from the reported IRS statistics.

18. This is the case with durable goods, such as new cars and major household appliances, as well as new homes and nondurable goods, such as food, clothing, gasoline, and so forth. For example, the consumption of meat (beef and pork), milk, eggs, sugar, potatoes, and canned fruits and vegetables all declined during the period 1970 to 1987, while consumers switched to cheaper fresh vegetables and chicken, whose consumption increased during this period (U.S. Bureau of the Census 1990, 124–25, 431).

19. This is not only the case with working-class families, but more and more middle-income professionals and owners of small family businesses are increasingly finding themselves in this predicament during this period of economic decline.

20. Total household debt in 1989 was over $3.3 trillion.

21. The nature and extent of poverty in the United States is discussed at some length later in this chapter.

22. An additional contributing factor to the inability to purchase a house or foreclosures due to the inability to make monthly mortgage payments has been

high interest rates, as they have increased from 5 or 6 percent in the 1950s and 1960s to about 10 percent in the 1970s and 1980s, even reaching 14 to 15 percent for a period in the early 1980s (U.S. Bureau of the Census 1990, 726).

23. During the period from 1970 to 1988 delinquency rates on VA and FHA loans have doubled, while foreclosure rates have tripled (U.S. Bureau of the Census 1990, 505).

24. These changes in the domestic labor force structure are taking place within the framework of changes in the international division of labor effected by the internationalization of U.S. capital and the transfer of the production process to low-wage areas overseas (see Chapter 4).

25. As pointed out earlier in this chapter, not only has affordable housing become difficult to obtain, but the amount of food consumption by workers has been declining relative to earlier periods.

26. Contrary to the prevailing myth, there are twice as many white people in poverty in the United States as there are black. If the near-poverty population is considered, we find three times as many whites in this category as blacks. Although given the much larger size of the total white population this should hardly come as a surprise, the common misconception that automatically identifies poverty with blacks and other minorities in general (rather than by class) has serious political implications affecting the entire working class—something that is recognized only by a handful of unionists in the labor movement.

27. We refer here to the qualitative shift in state policy during the Reagan administration in the 1980s as compared to the "welfare state" policies of both Democratic and Republican administrations of previous periods. Likewise, the top tax rate was reduced from 70 percent to 28 percent, as part of the tax cuts of 1981.

28. The reference here is to David Stockman's confessions on the real intentions of the Reagan administration's tax policies based on "supply-side economics," which Stockman identified as a "Trojan horse," while George Bush characterized it in 1980 as "voodoo economics."

29. The growth of the state, its spending and tax policies, budget deficits, and the mushrooming national debt over the past two decades are discussed below with data provided in Table 6.1 and Figures 6.1–6.3.

30. Prior to the passage of the 1986 tax reform act, corporate taxes dropped to an all-time low of 6.2 percent of total federal tax receipts in the mid-1980s.

31. It is in this sense that General Motors, for example, is able to shut down some two dozen plants in the United States—throwing many workers onto the unemployment lines—only to open new plants across the border in Mexico to cut down its wage bill and increase profits for its owners, while jeopardizing the lives of its workers and creating many other problems that impact the state and state policy.

32. The exact cost of the Gulf War is not yet clear. The administration was initially authorized to spend $15 billion, but it asked from Congress in early 1991 an allowance of $58 billion, with the understanding that a large portion

of this amount would be returned once the pledges of support from the allies were fulfilled. The total cost of the Gulf War for the United States alone (excluding all the destruction caused in Kuwait and Iraq) was, according to some estimates, upward of $86 billion as of March 1991, and a substantial portion of the allied pledges have yet to materialize. Given this, it is not unreasonable to assume that the final cost of the war to the U.S. taxpayers will probably exceed $50 billion. For further discussion on this see Griffen 1991.

33. See the various essays in Hall 1972 on corruption in these and other unions dominated by conservative, collaborationist top union officials.

34. This period of paralysis of organized labor is associated with the conservative turn in politics under the Reagan administration during the 1980s.

35. For an extended discussion of these structural changes in a broader global context, see Berberoglu 1987. Also see Peet 1987.

36. Table 7.1 and Figures 4.8, 5.1, and 6.3 reprinted with permission from *Dollars & Sense*, 1 Summer St., Somerville, MA 02143.

37. This was a major issue in the coal miners' strike in the early 1970s. When the union leadership tried to force a contract on the miners that contained a no-strike clause, it was overwhelmingly rejected.

38. The most prominent of these was the struggle for the 8-hour day in the late nineteenth century, when a number of labor leaders were executed over the Haymarket Affair. See Boyer and Morais 1980.

39. For further analysis of the implications of this experience for the current state of the labor movement in the United States, see Lembcke 1988.

40. At the national convention of the UE union in the early 1980s, for example, union officers stressed the necessity of independent political action through labor initiatives: "Only when the labor movement strengthens its own forces and builds up its own political party," the organizers proclaimed, "will we be successful in our fight to beat the Reagan reaction and to achieve an economic program that serves the people" (Spektor 1981, 4). Among the older leftist political parties and organizations are the Workers World party, the Socialist Workers party, the Communist Labor party, the Socialist party, and the Democratic Socialists, as well as the Communist Party USA and other political parties and organizations. Though they vary in their strategy and tactics and are linked with the working class in varying degrees, all of these organizations agree on the exploitative nature of capitalism and the need for its replacement by socialism—though here, too, defining socialism in different ways, while most of them agreeing that it is a type of state and society run by and in the interests of the working class.

References

Ackerman, Frank. 1982. *Reaganomics: Rhetoric vs. Reality.* Boston: South End Press.

Amott, Teresa. 1990. "A Recession by Any Other Name: Labels Aside, the Hard Times Are Here." *Dollars & Sense*, no. 162 (December).

Ayala, Cesar J. 1989. "Theories of Big Business in American Society." *Critical Sociology*, 16, no. 2–3 (Summer–Fall).

Baran, Paul A., and Paul M. Sweezy. 1966. *Monopoly Capital.* New York: Monthly Review Press.

Berberoglu, Berch. 1987. *The Internationalization of Capital: Imperialism and Capitalist Development on a World Scale.* New York: Praeger.

———. 1990. *Political Sociology: A Comparative/Historical Approach.* New York: General Hall.

———. 1992. *The Political Economy of Development: Development Theory and the Prospects for Change in the Third World.* Albany: State University of New York Press.

Bergman, Gregory. 1986. "The 1920s and the 1980s: A Comparison." *Monthly Review* 38, no. 5 (October).

Biro, Lajos, and Marc J. Cohen, eds. 1979. *The United States in Crisis.* Minneapolis: MEP Press.

Bluestone, Barry, and Bennett Harrison. 1982. *The Deindustrialization of America.* New York: Basic Books.

Bowles, Samuel, and Richard Edwards. 1985. *Understanding Capitalism.* New York: Harper & Row.

Boyer, Richard, and Herbert Morais. 1980. *Labor's Untold Story.* 3d ed. New York: United Electrical, Radio & Machine Workers of America.

Braun, Denny. 1991. *The Rich Get Richer: The Rise of Income Inequality in the United States and the World.* Chicago: Nelson Hall.

Campen, Jim. 1991. "The Second S&L Crisis." *Dollars & Sense,* no. 165 (April).

Cantor, Daniel, and Juliet Schor. 1987. *Tunnel Vision: Labor, the World Economy, and Central America.* Boston: South End Press.

Cappo, Joe. 1977. "A Little Closer Look at Free Enterprise." *Chicago Daily News* (May 17).

Cherry, Robert et al., eds. 1987. *The Imperiled Economy. Book I.* New York: Union for Radical Political Economics.

Curran, Daniel J., and Claire M. Ranzetti. 1990. *Social Problems: Society in Crisis.* 2d ed. Boston: Allyn and Bacon.

De Caux, Len. 1970. *Labor Radical.* Boston: Beacon Press.

_____. 1974. "UE: Democratic Unionism at Work." *World Magazine* (April).

Devine, Jim. 1982. "The Structural Crisis of U.S. Capitalism." *Southwest Economy and Society* 6, no. 1 (Fall).

Dollars & Sense. 1986. "The Politics of Homeownership," no. 114 (March).

Dowd, Douglas F. 1977. *The Twisted Dream: Capitalist Development in the United States since 1776.* Cambridge, MA: Winthrop.

Fajnzylber, Fernando. 1970. *Estrategia Industrial y Empresas Internacionales.* Rio de Janeiro: UN/CEPAL (November).

Fantasia, Rick. 1988. *Cultures of Solidarity: Consciousness, Action, and Contemporary American Workers.* Berkeley: University of California Press.

Feagin, Joe R., and Clairece Booher Feagin. 1990. *Social Problems: A Critical Power-Conflict Perspective.* 3d ed. Englewood Cliffs, NJ: Prentice Hall.

Feagin, Joe R., and Robert Parker. 1990. *Building American Cities.* 2d ed. Englewood Cliffs, NJ: Prentice Hall.

Fleming, D. F. 1961. *The Cold War and Its Origins, 1917–1960.* 2 vols. Garden City, NY: Doubleday.

Foster, John B. 1986. *The Theory of Monopoly Capitalism.* New York: Monthly Review Press.

Foster, John B., and Henryk Szlajfer, eds. 1984. *The Faltering Economy: The Problem of Accumulation Under Monopoly Capitalism.* New York: Monthly Review Press.

Gimenez, Martha. 1987. "The Feminization of Poverty: Myth or Reality." *The Insurgent Sociologist* 14, no. 3 (Fall).

Green, Gil. 1976. *What's Happening to Labor.* New York: International Publishers.

Greider, William. 1981. "The Education of David Stockman." *Atlantic Monthly* (December).

Griffen, Sarah. 1991. "The War Bill: Adding Up the Domestic Costs of War." *Dollars & Sense,* no. 165 (April).

Hall, Burton, ed. 1972. *Autocracy and Insurgency in Organized Labor.* New Brunswick, NJ: Transaction Books.

Halliday, John and Gavan McCormic. 1973. *Japanese Imperialism Today.* New York: Monthly Review Press.

Harrison, Bennett, and Barry Bluestone. 1988. *The Great U-Turn.* New York: Basic Books.

Harvey, David. 1982. *The Limits to Capital.* Chicago: University of Chicago Press.

Hopkins, Terence K., and Immanuel Wallerstein. 1981. "Structural Transformations of the World-Economy." In Richard Rubinson, eds., *Dynamics of World Development.* London: Sage Publications.

_____. 1982. *World-Systems Analysis.* Beverly Hills, CA: Sage Publications.

Howe, Irving, ed. 1972. *The World of the Blue Collar Worker.* New York: Quadrangle Books.

Institute for Labor Education and Research. 1982. *What's Wrong with the U.S. Economy?* Boston: South End Press.

Institute for Research on Poverty. 1987–88. "Tracking the Homeless." *Focus* (Winter).

Jenkins, Craig, and C. Eckert. 1989. "The Corporate Elite, the New Conservative Policy Network, and Reaganomics." *Critical Sociology* 16, no. 2–3 (Summer–Fall).

Katznelson, Ira, and Al Zolberg, eds. 1986. *Workingclass Formation: Nineteenth-century Patterns in Western Europe and the United States.* Princeton, NJ: Princeton University Press.

Keeran, Roger. 1980. *The Communist Party and the Auto Workers' Unions.* Bloomington: Indiana University Press.

Kennedy, Paul. 1987. *The Rise and Fall of the Great Powers.* New York: Random House.

Kidron, Michael. 1970. *Western Capitalism since the War.* Harmondsworth, England: Penguin Books.

Kimeldorf, Howard. 1988. *Reds or Rackets? The Making of Radical and Conservative Unions on the Waterfront.* Berkeley: University of California Press.

Kloby, Jerry. 1987. "The Growing Divide: Class Polarization in the 1980s." *Monthly Review* 39, no. 4 (September).

_____. 1988. "The Top-heavy Economy: Managerial Greed and Unproductive Labor." *Critical Sociology* 15, no. 3 (Fall).

_____. 1991. "Increasing Class Polarization in the United States: The Growth of Wealth and Income Inequality." In Berch Berberoglu, ed., *Critical Perspectives in Sociology: A Reader.* Dubuque, IA: Kendall/Hunt Publishing Company.

Larrowe, Charles P. 1972. *Harry Bridges: The Rise and Fall of Radical Labor in the U.S.* Westport, CT: Lawrence Hill.

Lembcke, Jerry. 1988. *Capitalist Development and Class Capacities: Marxist Theory and Union Organization.* Westport, CT: Greenwood Press.

Levenstein, Harvey. 1981. *Communism, Anticommunism, and the CIO*. Westport, CT: Greenwood Press.

Lewis, Cleona. 1938. *America's Stake in International Investments*. Washington, DC: Brookings Institution.

Liazos, Alexander. 1982. *People First: An Introduction to Social Problems*. Boston: Allyn and Bacon.

Lotta, Raymond. 1984. *America in Decline*, vol. 1. Chicago: Banner Press.

Magdoff, Harry, and Paul M. Sweezy. 1977. *The End of Prosperity: The American Economy in the 1970s*. New York: Monthly Review Press.

_____. 1981. *The Deepening Crisis of U.S. Capitalism*. New York: Monthly Review Press.

_____. 1987. *Stagnation and the Financial Explosion*. New York: Monthly Review Press.

Mandel, Ernest. 1978. *Late Capitalism*. London: Verso.

_____. 1980. *The Second Slump*. London: Verso.

Martin, Linda Grant. 1975. "The 500: A Report on Two Decades." *Fortune* (May).

Medlen, Craig. 1984. "Corporate Taxes and the Federal Deficit." *Monthly Review* 36, no. 6 (November).

Melendez, Edwin. 1988. "Reaganomics and Racial Inequality: A Decade of Lost Gains." *Dollars & Sense*, no. 137 (June).

Melman, Seymour. 1965. *Our Depleated Society*. New York: Holt, Rinehart and Winston.

_____. 1970. *Pentagon Capitalism: The Political Economy of War*. New York: McGraw-Hill Book Company.

Mermelstein, David, ed. 1975. *The Economic Crisis Reader*. New York: Vintage Books.

Meurs, Mieke. 1989. "Uncertain Harvest: The Making of the Next Farm Crisis." *Dollars & Sense*, no. 147 (June).

Miller, John A. 1987. "Accumulation and State Intervention in the 1980s: A Crisis of Reproduction." In Robert Cherry et al., eds., *The Imperiled Economy*. Book I. New York: Union for Radical Political Economics.

_____. 1989. "Helping the Rich Help Themselves: Bush Offers Capital-Gains Tax Giveaway." *Dollars & Sense*, no. 147 (June).

Moody, Kim. 1990. "The Bad Deal: Bargaining in the 1980's." *Labor Notes*, no. 130 (January).

Morris, George. 1971. *Rebellion in the Unions*. New York: New Outlook.

Nathanson, Charles E. 1969. "The Militarization of the American Economy." In David Horowitz, ed., *Corporations and the Cold War*. New York: Monthly Review Press.

Nissen, Bruce. 1981. "U.S. Workers and the U.S. Labor Movement." *Monthly Review* 33, no. 1 (May).

O'Connor, James. 1973. *The Fiscal Crisis of the State*. New York: St. Martin's Press.

_____. 1974. *The Corporations and the State*. New York: Harper & Row.

_____. 1984. *Accumulation Crisis*. New York: Basil Blackwell.

Parenti, Michael. 1989. *The Sword and the Dollar: Imperialism, Revolution, and the Arms Race*. New York: St. Martin's Press.

Parker, Robert E. 1991. "Urban Social Problems in the United States: Issues in Urban Political Economy." In Berch Berberoglu, ed., *Critical Perspectives in Sociology: A Reader*. Dubuque, IA: Kendall/Hunt Publishing Company.

Peet, Richard, ed. 1987. *International Capitalism and Industrial Restructuring*. Boston: Allen & Unwin.

Perlo, Victor. 1988. *Super Profits and Crises: Modern U.S. Capitalism*. New York: International Publishers.

Perrucci, Carolyn C., et al. 1988. *Plant Closings: International Context and Social Costs*. New York: Aldine de Gruyter.

Petras, James. 1978. *Critical Perspectives on Imperialism and Social Class in the Third World*. New York: Monthly Review Press.

_____. 1981. *Class, State and Power in the Third World*. Montclair, NJ: Allanheld, Osmun.

Petras, James, and Christian Bay. 1990. "The Changing Wealth of the U.S. Ruling Class." *Monthly Review* 42, no. 7 (December).

Pollin, Robert. 1990. "Borrowing More, Buying Less." *Dollars & Sense*, no. 156 (May).

Salt, James. 1989. "Sunbelt Capital and Conservative Political Realignment in the 1970s and 1980s." *Critical Sociology* 16, no. 2–3 (Summer–Fall).

Servan-Schreiber, J. J. 1968. *The American Challenge*. New York: Atheneum.

Sherman, Howard. 1976. *Stagflation*. New York: Harper & Row.

_____. 1987. *Foundations of Radical Political Economy*. Armonk, NY: M. E. Sharpe.

Shields, Lynn. 1988. "Endangered Species: The Uncertain Future of Low-Income Housing." *Dollars & Sense*, no. 141 (November).

Slaughter, Jane. 1990. "Is the Labor Movement Reaching a Turning Point?" *Labor Notes*, no. 130 (January).

Smith, Joan. 1981. *Social Issues and the Social Order: The Contradictions of Capitalism*. Cambridge, MA: Winthrop.

Spektor, C. 1981. "U. E. Convention Call: New Political Party Needed." *Peoples World* (September 26).

Stepan-Norris, Judith, and Maurice Zeitlin. 1989. " 'Who Gets the Bird?' or, How the Communists Won Power and Trust in America's Unions." *American Sociological Review* 54 (August).

Sweezy, Paul M., and Harry Magdoff. 1972. *The Dynamics of U.S. Capitalism*. New York: Monthly Review Press.

_____. 1988. "The Stock Market Crash and Its Aftermath." *Monthly Review* 39, no. 10 (March).

Szymanski, Albert. 1978. *The Capitalist State and the Politics of Class*. Cambridge, MA: Winthrop.

_____. 1981. *The Logic of Imperialism*. New York: Praeger.

Tanzer, Michael. 1974. *The Energy Crisis: World Struggle for Power and Wealth*. New York: Monthly Review Press.

Union for Radical Political Economics. 1978. *U.S. Capitalism in Crisis*. New York: Union For Radical Political Economics.

U.S. Bureau of the Census. 1975. *Statistical Abstract of the United States: 1975*. Washington, DC: Government Printing Office.

_____. 1981. *Statistical Abstract of the United States: 1981*. Washington, DC: Government Printing Office.

_____. 1987. *Statistical Abstract of the United States: 1987*. Washington, DC: Government Printing Office.

_____. 1988. *Statistical Abstract of the United States: 1988*. Washington, DC: Government Printing Office.

_____. 1990. *Statistical Abstract of the United States: 1990*. Washington, DC: Government Printing Office.

U.S. Council of Economic Advisers. 1990. *Economic Report of the President, 1990*. Washington, DC: Government Printing Office.

U.S. Department of Commerce. 1990. *Survey of Current Business* (August).

U.S. Office of Management and Budget. 1991. *Budget of the United States Government, Fiscal Year 1992*. Washington, DC: Government Printing Office.

Useem, Michael. 1989. "Revolt of the Corporate Owners and the Demobilization of Business Political Action." *Critical Sociology* 16, no. 2–3 (Summer–Fall).

Valvano, Vince. 1988. "No Longer #1? Assessing U.S. Economic Decline." *Dollars & Sense*, no. 142 (December).

Wallerstein, Immanuel. 1974a. "The Rise and Future Demise of the World Capitalist System." *Comparative Studies in Society and History* 16, no. 4 (September).

_____. 1974b. *The Modern World System*. New York: Academic Press.

_____. 1979. *The Capitalist World-Economy*. Cambridge: Cambridge University Press.

Warren, Bill. 1980. *Imperialism, Pioneer of Capitalism*. New York: Verso.

Weeks, John. 1981. *Capital and Exploitation*. Princeton, NJ: Princeton University Press.

Yates, Michael D. 1990. "From the Coal Wars to the Pittston Strike." *Monthly Review* 42, no. 2 (June).

Index

ABOUT THE AUTHOR

BERCH BERBEROGLU is Professor of Sociology at the University of Nevada, Reno. Dr. Berberoglu is the author of several books, including *The Internationalization of Capital: Imperialism and Capitalist Development on a World Scale* (Praeger, 1987), *Political Sociology: A Comparative/Historical Approach,* and *The Political Economy of Development: Development Theory and the Prospects for Change in the Third World.* His forthcoming book *The Labor Process and Control of Labor in Capitalist Society* promises to make an important contribution to sociology and labor studies. He is currently working on a new book, *The European and Japanese Challenge: Global Rivalry and the Rise of the Old Powers in the Late 20th Century.*